Innovation, Technology, and Knowledge Management

Series Editor

Elias G. Carayannis
George Washington University, Washington, DC, USA

For further volumes:
http://www.springer.com/series/8124

Martin Curley · Piero Formica
Editors

The Experimental Nature of New Venture Creation

Capitalizing on Open Innovation 2.0

 Springer

Editors
Martin Curley
Piero Formica
National University of Ireland Maynooth
Maynooth
Kildare
Ireland

ISBN 978-3-319-00178-4   ISBN 978-3-319-00179-1   (eBook)
DOI 10.1007/978-3-319-00179-1
Springer Cham Heidelberg New York Dordrecht London

Library of Congress Control Number: 2013939341

Springer is part of Springer Science+Business Media (www.springer.com)

*By achieving superior economics of experi-
mentation, a company can gain a simulation
advantage. An array of levers and behaviours
must be integrated and deployed to establish
a culture of experimentation. Companies with
a simulation advantage embrace change,
cultivate a hunger for information and
tolerate failure.*

The Boston Consulting Group

To our parents

Series Foreword

The Springer book series *Innovation, Technology, and Knowledge Management* was launched in March 2008 as a forum and intellectual, scholarly"podium" for global/local, transdisciplinary, transsectoral, public–private, and leading/"bleeding"-edge ideas, theories, and perspectives on these topics.

The book series is accompanied by the Springer *Journal of the Knowledge Economy*, which was launched in 2009 with the same editorial leadership.

The series showcases provocative views that diverge from the current "conventional wisdom" that are properly grounded in theory and practice, and that consider the concepts of **robust competitiveness**,[1] **sustainable entrepreneurship**,[2] and **democratic capitalism**,[3] central to its philosophy and objectives. More specifically, the aim of this series is to highlight emerging research and practice at the dynamic intersection of these fields, where individuals, organizations, industries, regions, and nations are harnessing creativity and invention to achieve and sustain growth.

---

[1] We define *sustainable entrepreneurship* as the creation of viable, profitable, and scalable firms. Such firms engender the formation of self-replicating and mutually enhancing innovation networks and knowledge clusters (innovation ecosystems), leading toward robust competitiveness (E. G. Carayannis, *International Journal of Innovation and Regional Development* 1(3), 235–254, 2009).

[2] We understand *robust competitiveness* to be a state of economic being and becoming that avails systematic and defensible "unfair advantages" to the entities that are part of the economy. Such competitiveness is built on mutually complementary and reinforcing low-, medium-, and high-technology and public and private sector entities (government agencies, private firms, universities, and nongovernmental organizations) (E. G. Carayannis, *International Journal of Innovation and Regional Development* 1(3), 235–254, 2009).

[3] The concepts of *robust competitiveness and sustainable entrepreneurship* are pillars of a regime that we call "*democratic capitalism*" (as opposed to "popular or casino capitalism"), in which real opportunities for education and economic prosperity are available to all, especially—but not only—younger people. These are the direct derivatives of a collection of top-down policies as well as bottom-up initiatives (including strong research and development policies and funding, but going beyond these to include the development of innovation networks and knowledge clusters across regions and sectors) (E. G. Carayannis and A. Kaloudis, *Japan Economic Currents*, p. 6–10 January 2009).

Books that are part of the series explore the impact of innovation at the "macro" (economies, markets), "meso" (industries, firms), and "micro" levels (teams, individuals), drawing from such related disciplines as finance, organizational psychology, research and development, science policy, information systems, and strategy, with the underlying theme that for innovation to be useful it must involve the sharing and application of knowledge.

Some of the key anchoring concepts of the series are outlined in the figure below and the definitions that follow (all definitions are from E. G. Carayannis and D. F. J. Campbell, *International Journal of Technology Management*, 46, 3–4, 2009).

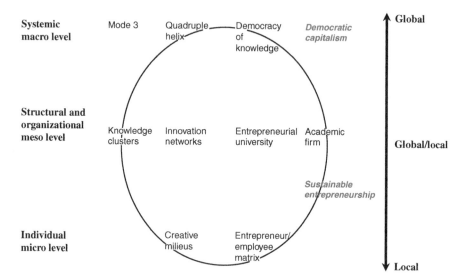

Conceptual profile of the series *Innovation, Technology,* and *Knowledge Management*

- The "Mode 3" Systems Approach for Knowledge Creation, Diffusion, and Use: "Mode 3" is a multilateral, multinodal, multimodal, and multilevel systems approach to the conceptualization, design, and management of real and virtual, "knowledge-stock" and "knowledge-flow," modalities that catalyze, accelerate, and support the creation, diffusion, sharing, absorption, and use of cospecialized knowledge assets. "Mode 3" is based on a system-theoretic perspective of socioeconomic, political, technological, and cultural trends and conditions that shape the coevolution of knowledge with the "knowledge-based and knowledge-driven, global/local economy and society."
- Quadruple Helix: Quadruple helix, in this context, means to add to the triple helix of government, university, and industry a "fourth helix" that we identify as the "media-based and culture-based public." This fourth helix associates with "media," "creative industries," "culture," "values," "life styles," "art," and perhaps also the notion of the "creative class."

- Innovation Networks: Innovation networks are real and virtual infrastructures and infratechnologies that serve to nurture creativity, trigger invention, and catalyze innovation in a public and/or private domain context (for instance, government–university–industry public–private research and technology development coopetitive partnerships).
- Knowledge Clusters: Knowledge clusters are agglomerations of cospecialized, mutually complementary, and reinforcing knowledge assets in the form of "knowledge stocks" and "knowledge flows" that exhibit self-organizing, learning-driven, dynamically adaptive competences, and trends in the context of an open systems perspective.
- Twenty-First Century Innovation Ecosystem: A twenty-first century innovation ecosystem is a multilevel, multimodal, multinodal, and multiagent system of systems. The constituent systems consist of innovation metanetworks (networks of innovation networks and knowledge clusters) and knowledge metaclusters (clusters of innovation networks and knowledge clusters) as building blocks and organized in a self-referential or chaotic fractal knowledge and innovation architecture,[4] which in turn constitute agglomerations of human, social, intellectual, and financial capital stocks and flows as well as cultural and technological artifacts and modalities, continually coevolving, cospecializing, and cooperating. These innovation networks and knowledge clusters also form, reform, and dissolve within diverse institutional, political, technological, and socioeconomic domains, including government, university, industry, and nongovernmental organizations and involving information and communication technologies, biotechnologies, advanced materials, nanotechnologies, and next-Generation energy technologies.

Who is this book series published for? The book series addresses a diversity of audiences in different settings:

1. *Academic communities*: Academic communities worldwide represent a core group of readers. This follows from the theoretical/conceptual interest of the book series to influence academic discourses in the fields of knowledge, also carried by the claim of a certain saturation of academia with the current concepts and the postulate of a window of opportunity for new or at least additional concepts. Thus, it represents a key challenge for the series to exercise a certain impact on discourses in academia. In principle, all academic communities that are interested in knowledge (knowledge and innovation) could be tackled by the book series. The interdisciplinary (transdisciplinary) nature of the book series underscores that the scope of the book series is not limited a priori to a specific basket of disciplines. From a radical viewpoint, one could create the hypothesis that there is no discipline where knowledge is of no importance.
2. *Decision makers—private/academic entrepreneurs and public (governmental, subgovernmental) actors*: Two different groups of decision makers are being

---

[4] E. G. Carayannis, *Strategic Management of Technological Learning*, CRC Press, 2000.

addressed simultaneously: (1) private entrepreneurs (firms, commercial firms, academic firms) and academic entrepreneurs (universities), interested in optimizing knowledge management and in developing heterogeneously composed knowledge-based research networks; and (2) public (governmental, subgovernmental) actors that are interested in optimizing and further developing their policies and policy strategies that target knowledge and innovation. One purpose of public *knowledge and innovation policy* is to enhance the performance and competitiveness of advanced economies.

3. *Decision makers in general*: Decision makers are systematically being supplied with crucial information, for how to optimize knowledge-referring and knowledge-enhancing decision-making. The nature of this "crucial information" is conceptual as well as empirical (case-study-based). Empirical information highlights practical examples and points toward practical solutions (perhaps remedies), conceptual information offers the advantage of further driving and further-carrying tools of understanding. Different groups of addressed decision makers could be decision makers in private firms and multinational corporations, responsible for the knowledge portfolio of companies; knowledge and knowledge management consultants; globalization experts, focusing on the internationalization of research and development, science and technology, and innovation; experts in university/business research networks; and political scientists, economists, and business professionals.

4. *Interested global readership*: Finally, the Springer book series addresses a whole global readership, composed of members who are generally interested in knowledge and innovation. The global readership could partially coincide with the communities as described above ("academic communities," "decision makers"), but could also refer to other constituencies and groups.

Elias G. Carayannis
Series Editor

Foreword

This book, *The Experimental Nature of New Venture Creation,* edited by Martin Curley and Piero Formica consists of a collection of very insightful as well as inciteful chapters in trying to open the "black box" of entrepreneurial endeavor and the nature and dynamics of the innovation process.

This book will make a valuable contribution for both practitioners as well as policy makers to more effectively trigger, catalyze, and accelerate high quality as well as quantity innovation via more structured and systematic learning-facilitating experiments.

The book series of which this book will be part, along with the other publication projects for which I am the founding editor, such as the Springer *Innovation, Technology and Knowledge Management* Series, as well as the related Springer *Journal of the Knowledge Economy,* Springer *Journal of Innovation and Entrepreneurship* and the Springer *Encyclopedia of Creativity, Invention, Innovation and Entrepreneurship,* form part of a combination of projects aiming at advancing the state of the art in the understanding and facilitating the heart of sustainable, intelligent, and inclusive growth.

Elias G. Carayannis
George Washington University

Preface

This book gives us cause to fundamentally re-evaluate the processes of innovation and entrepreneurship, and to rethink how they might best be stimulated and fostered within our organisations and communities. The fundamental thesis of the book is that the entrepreneurial process is not a linear progression from novel idea to successful innovation, but is an iterative series of experiments, where progress depends on the persistence and resilience of the individuals involved, and their ability and to learn from failure as well as success. From this, the authors argue that the ideal environment for new venture creation is a form of 'experimental laboratory', a community of innovators where ideas are generated, shared and refined, experiments are encouraged, and which in itself serves as a test environment for those ideas and experiments. This environment is quite different from the traditional 'incubator', which may impose the disciplines of the established firm too early in the development of the new venture.

Innovation and entrepreneurship are much discussed by those involved in education, enterprise and the development of public policy, driven by the assertion that the comparative advantage of nations no longer depends merely on their means of production, but on their capacity to create and assimilate knowledge, their ability to envision new ways of doing things, the speed with which they adopt and adapt to these innovations, and the rate at which they generate new and enhanced artefacts, services, goods and products that are sought after by others. While there is an extensive descriptive literature of the processes involved in innovation and entrepreneurship, it does not seem to be fully appreciated just how complex, extraordinary and vulnerable these processes are, especially when full consideration is given to cognitive and social processes underpinning innovation, and the institutional and cultural contexts in which they occur.

The process of innovation is all the more extraordinary when we consider just how much of what we do is habitual: we are quite literally creatures of habit. We normally respond to stimuli and problems with habitual learned responses. This is not surprising. These responses have proved effective, to us or to others, in the past, so we use or adapt these learned responses as any new challenge unfolds. Nor is it inappropriate, as these learned responses are often the optimum solutions within current knowledge, technology and social structures. Moreover, the stability of society depends on some level of predictability in social interaction, so that such learned responses are expressed as norms of behaviour. It is an important function of learning and culture to transmit such tried and tested responses and solutions from generation to generation, maintaining complex social structures and relieving us of the need to reinvent the wheel.

Given the centrality of habitual action and learned responses in our behaviour, what is remarkable is that individuals and groups actually do question established norms, envision new approaches, act to change the way things are done, and to drive others to adopt these ways of doing and being. It is all the more remarkable when we consider the extent and strength of social and cultural forces that tend to suppress innovation. Nonetheless, innovation occurs, on a considerable scale, and it is worth considering the social and cultural conditions which foster innovation. These include free access to knowledge, openness to questioning, protection for the questioner and the contrary view, tolerance of difference and dissent, high levels of autonomy and capacity for independent action, and acceptance of risk.

These characteristics can be said to be present to a greater or lesser extent in any social group or culture, and it can be argued that where they are present, the capacity for innovation is greatest. However, these are not fixed characteristics of a social group, they can vary with context, so that in different contexts, the same social group can be more or less tolerant of difference, allow greater or lesser autonomy, or be more or less accepting of risk.

There are two particular contexts where the social characteristics of innovation are very strongly expressed: play and experimentation. These are contexts where questioning, difference, autonomy, action, imagination and innovation are strongly reinforced, in a context where the risks associated with these behaviours are accepted or controlled. Play and experimentation are inter-related: play involves exploratory and experimental activities, there are distinguished scientists who argue that experimentation has playful characteristics, and distinguished educators who argue that play and experimentation are intrinsic to learning.

Against this backdrop, the idea that a new form of 'experimental laboratory' is the optimum environment for new ventures to germinate and blossom is timely and compelling. This volume explores the experimental nature of new venture creation, develops the idea of formally structuring and supporting such experimentation in a 'new venture laboratory' setting, considers the role of universities and other knowledge organisations in establishing an 'ecosystem' in which such experimental approaches can thrive, and draws on the experience of students and practitioners to describe such 'experimental laboratories' in action.

This book is a clarion call to those in academia, enterprise and government who seek to work together to promote innovation and entrepreneurship, with a stark message for academic institutions: engage or be left behind. Higher education institutions, and in particular universities, have emphasised the generation, dissemination and conservation of knowledge over its exploitation and application. Furthermore, research universities no longer have a monopoly on generating knowledge or educating people, and a wide variety of enterprises, economic and social, can be seen as knowledge enterprises, discovering, applying and teaching.

The university of the future will not be an isolated institution, but a vital node in a fluid network of interdependent knowledge organisations which together create an innovation system. This requires universities to rethink their structures and processes, enterprise to re-evaluate their conceptions of value, risk and return, and governments, through regulation and funding, to promote an intimate and mutually beneficial interaction between public universities and private knowledge enterprises. This book is an essential reading for those willing and able to think anew about these critical relationships.

Prof. Philip Nolan
President, National University of Ireland
Maynooth
Ireland

Acknowledgments

The ideas for this book were starting to come together during our lectures held at the International Entrepreneurship Academy. We owe Professors Thomas Andersson, former President of Jönköping University and Niclas Adler, former Dean of Jönköping International Business School, a debt of gratitude for having provided anecdotes about business historians plunged into case studies and business economists who are familiar with the field known as experimental economics. Those narratives led to the book's title.

We are grateful to the many insightful comments we have received from our colleagues at the Innovation Value Institute (IVI). We want to extend particular thanks to Elias Carayannis (Full Professor of Science, Technology, Innovation and Entrepreneurship, at the School of Business of the George Washington University in Washington, DC.), Philip Nolan and Ray O'Neill (respectively, President of the National University of Ireland, Maynooth, and Vice President for Research).

A special debt of gratitude is owed to John Edmondson, Editor-In-Chief of Industry and Higher Education—UK, for his professional editing of our preliminary studies on the subject of this book published in his Journal, and to our editor at Springer for having offered guidance and suggestions throughout the publication process.

Maynooth, Ireland November 2012

Contents

Chapter 1
Introduction

Martin Curley and Piero Formica

> *Venture capitalist Jonathan Murray of Early Stage Partners described the startup process as a series of iterative experiments rather than a linear projection. Rather than writing a business plan with cash flow projections that have little or no basis in reality, Jonathan suggests approaching a startup as a series of experiments—a careful balance between objectivity and entrepreneurial zeal.*

Gary Schoeniger, Founder and CEO, The Entrepreneurial Learning Initiative.
In his masterpiece published in the decade preceding World War II, during the most severe economic depression of the twentieth century, John Maynard Keynes wrote,

> *…..there has been a chronic tendency throughout human history for the propensity to save to be stronger than the inducement to invest. The weakness of the inducement to invest has been at all times the key to the economic problem. To-day the explanation of the weakness of this inducement may chiefly lie in the extent of existing accumulations; whereas, formerly, risks and hazards of all kinds may have played a larger part. But the result is the same.*

M. Curley · P. Formica (✉)
Innovation Value Institute, National University of Ireland, Maynooth, Co. Kildare, Ireland
e-mail: piero.formica@gmail.com

M. Curley
Intel Labs Europe, Collinstown Business Park, Leixlip, Co. Kildare, Ireland
e-mail: martin.g.curley@intel.com

P. Formica
Master in Entrepreneurship and Technology Management, University of Tartu, Tartu, Estonia

International Entrepreneurship Academy, Via Altaseta 3, 40123 Bologna, Italy

M. Curley and P. Formica (eds.), *The Experimental Nature of New Venture Creation*,
Innovation, Technology, and Knowledge Management, DOI: 10.1007/978-3-319-00179-1_1,
© Springer International Publishing Switzerland 2013

The desire of the individual to augment his personal wealth by abstaining from consumption has usually been stronger than the inducement to the entrepreneur to augment the national wealth by employing labour on the construction of durable assets (Keynes 1936).

In view of the obstacles to world economic growth provided by the Great, Global Recession during the early twenty-first century, risks and hazards come back to the forefront among the factors that hamper business investment. The aspiring entrepreneurs more than the incumbents are having to cross the uncharted waters of the strait between the 'Scylla' of running a calculating risk or, worse, taking it and the 'Charybdis' of uncertainty about their entrepreneurial endeavours.

In this book we argue that experiments in and for new venture creation are an effective vehicle for crossing that strait. Experimentation is like yeast that raises the propensity for entrepreneurship and in this way helps to strengthen the inducement to invest in new ventures. Therefore, approaching a start-up as a series of experiments is both a guideline method and a consensus practice for hardening that soft underbelly of the economy that are productive investments.

The physical economy is gradually giving way to the digital economy.[1] This puts entrepreneurial start-ups under the pressure of a changing landscape. From incubators to accelerators and experimental labs, a broad range of start-up nurseries work to lower that pressure. As shown in the case of Philips InnoHub (den Ouden et al. 2008), their evolution takes place along the trajectories traced by open innovation setting, casual interactions between and fusion of people with different backgrounds and varied expertise.

Although seed and early stage funds are slipping, multiple and cheaper digital technologies trim down start-up costs and offer more options for budding entrepreneurs. Vigilant observation of the facts under the realism of assumptions—what we call 'entrepreneurship through experimentation'—helps knock down barriers that prevent potential entrepreneurs from exercising novel ideas ("something that is not fully formed and represents some radically different, disruptive concept"—Phillips 2009) and thereby increase the chances for an increasing number of young innovative companies to get off the ground.

New business ideas are brought to entrepreneurial execution through people, process, organisation and delivery. However, being subject to a high degree of uncertainty,[2] novelty makes people uncomfortable as to the launch of an entrepre-

---

[1] The physical economy brought forth the Agricultural Revolution, which "initiated a seizure of the means of organic production", and the Industrial Revolution, which "absorbed the means of mechanical production". The digital economy complies with the spirit of the Information Revolution, which "integrated the means of symbolic production", and the "post-symbolic Virtual Revolution, [which] is far more profound than any of these earlier disruptions, for it seizes the means of perception itself—the very means of cognition" (Gargett 2001).

[2] Robert Skidelsky, biographer of John Manard Keynes, points out that "Keynes was the first economist to put uncertainty at the heart of the economic problems and thus raise the issue of the scope and meaning of rationality in economics......Keynes claimed that the mind could often 'reduce' uncertainty tp probability, 'intuiting' that some outcomes are more or less likely that others; in his words, 'perceiving a probability relation between the evidence (the premiss) and the conclusion of an argument" (Skidelsky 2010).

neurial initiative. Stepping outside the bounds of safety means to recognise and accept a culture of how to handle uncertain expectations that, all other things equal, interfere with the ability to recognise a novel idea.

How to build such a culture through the broad window opened by experimentation in and for entrepreneurship is the subject matter of this book.

New ventures are deliberate and careful human creations. As products of inventive efforts, start-ups show that there is a direct link between the entrepreneur and the innovation process. Innovation is knowledge turned into action through creative endeavour that hugely depends on the willingness of individuals to start new companies. Thus, entrepreneurialism accelerates the innovation process by increasing the opportunities for the successful commercialisation of innovation.

These man-made artifices are primarily designed by experimenting how to put people together. To perform an experiment, a treatment must be administered to experimental units. In this book, the "units" we are concerned with are entrepreneurial teams. By conducting realistic experiments and/or reproducing the conditions of a situation or process, those teams can take a run along the business idea spectrum—from learning what the market wants[3] to ascertaining the needs and desires of consumers and developing products their customers may not know they need (Phillips 2009 and Fig. 3 in Chap. 4). Thus, effective innovation originates from the activity of matching innovative solutions with problems and opportunities detected in both the actual markets (market watch exercise) and the future markets (market foresight). Its sound reputation emanates not from selling ready-made solutions, but from the mastery of tailoring innovation to the current demands and potential needs of customers.

Effective innovation is entrepreneurial and entrepreneurial execution is an *atomic reaction* (see Chap. 6),[4] fully adequate if the innovation agent is an entrepreneur with enough energetic power, persistence, and disciplined fantasy[5] in utilising time and brainpower to create a pathway for an idea's success. Viewed from this perspective, effective innovation is an expedition with specific assignments such as *why* innovating; *what* kind of innovative concept (evolutionary or revolutionary) in product, service or business model; *which* criteria should the innovation satisfy; *who* and *where* is the target group; and *when* is the market-entry time.

---

[3] "The Googly thing is to launch [products] early on the Google Labs and then iterate, learning what the market wants—and making it great. The beauty of experimenting in this way is that you never get too far from what the market wants. The market pulls you back" (Salter 2008).

[4] Benoit Mandelbrot, a French American mathematician, stated that "a large part of economic theory is just physics with the words changed" (quoted from Skildesky 2009).

[5] One can argue that discipline and fantasy are two contradictory terms, which only appear because the world of innovation is populated by oxymora. From the perspective of cognitive science, that contradiction is only apparent since "our mind's constructions are one form of a disciplined fantasy" (Davies and Hoffman 2002—http://www.cogsci.uci.edu/~ddhoff/TopicRealityCheck.pdf).

Under stressful changes in science and technology as well as in academic business models, the 'ivory tower' universities of the Second Millennium give way to "university ecosystems" which design creative spaces for experimentation-based approaches to new ventures focused on innovation. The formation of university ecosystems conducive to cross-disciplinary experimentation spaces where interdependent partners from academia and business communities are put together in a very free environment is the subject of Chap. 2.

The role of universities is changing. In the last century, the primary focus areas of universities were education and research with key goals of creating and diffusing information and knowledge. Now, a third and equally important role, expectation and responsibility is emerging—that of value creation. Value in this context refers to both business value and societal value. With increasing scrutiny of funding into the third-level sector, governments and the public alike are expecting more accountability and proof of added value from universities. The use of a *University Ecosystem* approach can unleash much of the potential energy in universities and transform it into kinetic energy, with graduates not just emerging in a state of readiness to be an employee, but often as highly motivated entrepreneurs with business or social innovation initiatives in flight. An ecosystem can be defined as a network of interdependent organisations or people in a specific environment with partly shared perspectives, resources, aspirations and directions. The ecosystems with the biggest critical mass and the greatest velocity will have the most linear momentum and will ultimately win. This form of new posture equates to what Etzkowitz (2004) and Andersson et al. (2010) term the entrepreneurial university.

New venture creation takes place within human–human and human–technology interactions. Experiencing interactions as they occur in real life is in the nature of business creation. In the Chap. 3 we discuss the emergence of a powerful new paradigm—Open Innovation 2.0 (OI 2.0) which generates synergies and network effects. Capitalizing on OI 2.0 is unparalleled opportunity for aspiring entrepreneurs who perform experiments in high-expectation entrepreneurship.

The Chap. 4 introduces and explains the importance of high-expectation start-ups, which are firms launched by entrepreneurs with high ambitions for growth. The encounter between new technology and entrepreneurship that characterises such new ventures has a significant impact on the nature and speed of economic development, driving the growth of high-technology industries and helping to make the economic system open, complex and adaptive. Thus high-expectation entrepreneurship deserves special attention in entrepreneurship education.

Using an approach borrowed from both experimental scientific research and the practice of medicine, we propose a form of "business idea testing" and "entrepreneur training" in a laboratory environment. The ability to transpose, test and iterate new ideas and models in a business laboratory has significant potential in terms of promoting rapid learning and the preliminary validation of a new business idea—thus cutting risk, reducing cost and maximising the revenue potential. We argue that this approach is far more appropriate for entrepreneurship development in the new economic environment than the one of traditional business education models.

The Chap. 5 articulates the opportunity of using an experimental business laboratory approach as a means of accelerating the creation, incubation and testing of new venture ideas. Such a strategy leads to the establishment of a micro-ecosystem of aspiring entrepreneurs and others in a business laboratory environment. The goal is to create a mini idea-supercollider, in which a microscopic 'Medici Effect' can be achieved, between aspiring entrepreneurs with different ideas, experiences and disciplines meeting in a spirit of open innovation—the whole being much greater than the sum of its parts.

The development of an ecosystem for idea generation and rapid testing using business simulation tools can accelerate the creation, mobilisation and diffusion stages of the knowledge life cycle in a knowledge-driven entrepreneurship venture, while de-risking potential ventures before significant capital is applied.

In the Chap. 6 our discourse revolves around distinctions between the incubator and the experimental lab. Incubators are embedded in the culture of the economics of (value-added) services. To date, at least in Europe, they have operated in a manner analogous to the generation of nuclear power; that is, attempting to produce 'entrepreneurial energy' through a process of fission that creates a division between the aspiring entrepreneurs' demands for, and the corresponding supply of, support and services. The process has been artificially fuelled by the provision of subsidies and grants from the European Union and elsewhere. However, the outcomes, in terms of high-expectation start-ups and their long-term sustainability, have been mediocre. As Tamásy (2007, p. 460), Heisenberg Research Fellow at the School of Geography, Geology and Environmental Science, University of Auckland, concurs, "empirical research evidence clearly suggests that [incubators] tend to fail in supporting entrepreneurship, innovation, and regional development and, therefore, they do not fulfil their expected role as policy instrument". In contrast, experience in the USA—where the incubation process has been more successful, qualitatively, than in Europe—points to a new route: that of 'proof of concept', of which the Kauffman Foundation is the strongest advocate.

We can use the concept of nuclear fusion—not yet a commercial reality for the generation of power—as a metaphor for the present situation regarding entrepreneurial innovation. On the one hand, there is the failure of incubators and, on the other, the need to expand the incubation process beyond the limits of the business plan,[6] to encompass experimentation and the simulation of new business concepts

---

[6] Steve Blank, serial entrepreneur and professor of entrepreneurship, argues, "Entrepreneurs treat a business plan, once written, as a final collection of facts. Once completed you don't often hear about people rewriting their plan. Instead it is treated as the culmination of everything they know and believe. It's static". Blank often says about start-ups in particular, "No business plan survives first contact with customers". In Blank's view, a valid alternative to the business plan is the business models which "describes how your company creates, delivers and captures value".(http://www.innov8rs.org/resources/business-plans-dead-startup-guide-to-business-model-canvas/).

in an experimental laboratory environment. Such experimental labs are attuned to and conversant with the economics of experimentation. This proposed innovative shift requires the fusion (that is, in the terminology of nuclear physics, production of a single, heavier nucleus) rather than the separation or fission (production of several lighter nuclei), of the demand for and supply of experimentation—of which the services currently provided are only a part.

Lao Tsu said: "A journey of a thousand miles begins with a single step". In the Chap. 7, we argue that experiencing experiments is the first step aspiring entrepreneurs have to make. Innovation is impeded by path dependencies. To be effective, innovation requires a willingness to move into new and often unknown territories. Due to high levels of complexity and uncertainty of the innovation process, collaborative teams are much better than siloed teams at supporting the effectiveness of innovation at both micro and macro scales. Collaborative teams are nurtured by Gulliver-type experimenters who gain new insights by sharing and learning from each other in an experimental laboratory—resulting in a dynamic, adaptive ecosystem that creates, channels and transforms ideas into effective innovation via the continuous formation of relationships among aspiring entrepreneurs.

To blaze new paths, to try something new, an innovative act or procedure for the purpose of nurturing high-expectation start-ups: this is the mission business experimental labs pursue. Any experiment conducted therein is a step-wise process of creating, probing, testing and scrutinising business ideas and thinking. The end of each stage is a gain in experiential learning. Through learning by doing, direct experience and observation, interaction with peers and other active experimenters, both experts and non-experts, the aspiring entrepreneur makes and derives meanings about relevance, practicability and profitability of the business idea under experimental investigation. Of critical importance are rapid learning cycles. The transformational result is an idea turned into a start-up with a commercially scalable business model.

The Chap. 8"[7] demonstrates how Curley and Formica's model of the experimental laboratory for would-be entrepreneurs responds to the new business environment and the new thinking. The exploitation of knowledge and experience is increasingly important to companies operating in the globalised economy, faced with intense competition and striving to make headway in difficult markets. If such exploitation is important for existing companies, able to develop their own knowledge from previous experience, it is critical for new ventures which have no direct real-world experience on which to draw. Would-be entrepreneurs now operate in a very different business environment from that of their predecessors and they need new forms of entrepreneurship education and new methods of pre-launch trial and analysis for start-ups. The transition from 'nature' to 'nurture' in

---

[7] Chapters 8, 9 and 10 reflect the experience gained during the authors' time as students of the International Entrepreneurship Academy while at Jönköping University.

the approach to and perception of entrepreneurship, coupled with the increasingly engaged economic role of higher education institutions and research centres can be manipulated effectively to improve the prospects for success of high-expectation entrepreneurs.

A database providing information about previous start-ups is the subject of the Chap. 9. It could be of great use to the would-be entrepreneur and would enhance the value of the experimental phase. The database would give instant access to information that would contribute to the experimental process. Ready access to the histories of previous start-ups would help new entrepreneurs to learn from the successes and failures of others. In this respect it would increase their chances of turning their ambitious business ideas into practical realities outside the simulation bubble.

The demand for knowledge from high-expectation entrepreneurs is currently not being met by the supply of available knowledge from experts. The 'experimental lab' process is regarded as coming to an end when the idea has been thoroughly tested and is ready for launch into the marketplace. However, some uncertainties remain about the nature of the proposed process, especially with regard to the precise means adopted to achieve the final aim. The Chap. 10 considers the key role of the 'venture-sitter' in an experimental business laboratory. Venture-sitters are experts who, mirroring the approach of the baby-sitter, aim to obtain the trust of other experts (the 'relatives') and aspiring entrepreneurs (the 'parents') while looking after the new entrepreneurial idea (the 'child') to ensure that it is nurtured and developed in the best way possible.

Te Chap. 11 describes experiments in entrepreneurship training and new venture creation using the Entrepreneurship Home® methodology based on the entrepreneurial process and social constructivist approach to learning. The original model was created to describe the methodology. The stages of entrepreneurial process Idea generation, Opportunity recognition, Opportunity development and Venture launch are defined via *silos* Propositions, Idea development, Concept development and Business development containing intermediate mental and physical shape. Three venture creation experiment case studies in the field of hi-tech, creative and social entrepreneurship demonstrated similar patterns of entrepreneurial processes and relevance to the model.

New venture experiments can be incubated in an innovation network designed to spin out new ventures when they are ready to be successful. The *Wikipedia* ecosystem, highlighted in the chapter Wikipedia: Harnessing Collaborative Intelligence, manifests *collaborative intelligence* and serves as a model of how innovation networks can spawn new venture creation. Experiments can be incubated in an innovation network designed to spin out new ventures when they are ready to be successful. *Wikipedia* offers a model of how diverse experiments under the umbrella of a grand vision can lead to innovation. *Wikipedia* grew out of several unsuccessful for-profit experiments and has since spun off successful for-profit enterprises, becoming an exemplar of how a visionary, non-profit idea can spawn effective innovation leading to entrepreneurship and new venture creation. *Wikipedia* attracts diverse expertise into a shared problem-solving ecosystem, tapping the unique knowledge of contributors with different priorities, information and methods.

Recently, *'business model'* and *'business model innovation'* have gained substantial attention in the management literature and practice. However, many firms lack the capability to develop a novel business model to capture the value from new technologies and market opportunities. The existing literature on business model innovation highlights the central role of *'customer value'*. Further, it suggests that firms need to experiment with different business models and engage in *'trail-and-error'* learning when participating in business model innovation. Trial-and-error processes and prototyping with tangible artefacts are a fundamental characteristic of design.

The Chap. 13 explores the role of design-led innovation in facilitating firms to conceive and prototype novel and meaningful business models. It provides a brief review of the conceptual discussion on business model innovation and highlights the opportunities for linking it with the research stream of design-led innovation. Design-led business model innovation is proposed as a future research area and the role of design-led prototyping and new types of artefacts and prototypes' play within it are highlighted.

In making interbreeding between innovation process and design thinking, a company can exploit new business opportunities and create a better end user experience. Set forth in the Chap. 14, this is the case of Shimmer Research which has utilised experimental approaches to deliver accelerated growth. Shimmer's development path and varied revenue streams straddle both research/academic markets as well as more scaled commercial segments. We lay out the context and practical reasoning driving a fluid approach and describe specific examples of experimentation that led to product launch and refinement. By first building an ecosystem within the research field, the company was positioned as an innovative partner of the world's leading academic and clinical researchers. From that foundation, Shimmer has gone on to develop products for a variety of healthcare and sports applications and the Shimmer platform is now used in over 50 countries and continues to experiment to this day.

References

Andersson, T., Curley, G. M., & Formica, P. (2010). *Knowledge-driven entrepreneurship: the key to social and economic transformation*. New York: Springer.

Davies, T.M., & Hoffman, D.D. (2002). *"Reality check: insights from cognitive science"*. Topic, *1*(2), 102-105.

Den Ouden, E., Ee, D., Goh, N., (2008). The Philips innohub—generating breakthrough innovation in an open innovation setting. *PDMA Visions Magazine. 32*(1), 20–21.

Etzkowitz, H. (2004). The evolution of the entrepreneurial university. *International Journal of Technology and Globalisation, 1*(1), 64–77.

Gargett, A. (2001). Virtual spaces. *The Journal of Cognitive Liberties, 2*(3), 9–29.

Keynes, J. M. (1936). *The general theory of employment, interest and money*, London: Macmillan Cambridge University Press, for the Royal Economic Society.

Phillips, J. (2009). The idea spectrum. Innovate on Purpose, blog, March 21.
Salter, C., (2008, february and 19). Marissa Mayer's 9 principles of innovation—Google's VP of search products and user experience shares the rules that gives the search company its innovative edge. *Fast Company*. (http://www.fastcompany.com/article/marissa-mayer039s-9-principles-innovation).
Skidelski, R. (2009). *Keynes: the return of the master*. New York: Public Affairs.
Skidelsky, R. (2010). *Keynes: a very short introduction*. New York: Oxford University Press.
Tamàsy, C. (2007). Rethinking technology-oriented business incubators: developing a robust policy instrument for entrepreneurship, innovation, and regional development? *Growth and Change*, 6(3), 460–473.

Part I
Entrepreneurship as Experiment:
Socioeconomic Foundations

Chapter 2
University Ecosystems Design Creative Spaces for Start-Up Experimentation

Martin Curley and Piero Formica

> *When the winds of change come, some people build walls, other build windmills.*
> Brian and Sangeeta Mayne, Founders of Lift International.

Introduction

Religious roots marked the medieval university, *alma mater* of the Second Millennium higher education institutions. For centuries, the *'ivory tower'* syndrome, a reminiscence of their monastic lineage, has affected academic institutions. Einstein said, "The intuitive mind is a sacred gift and the rational mind is a faithful servant. We have created universities (society) that honors the servant and has forgotten the gift". This kind of thinking pervaded, limiting the scope of some universities to knowledge and student production. It seems that analysis has

M. Curley · P. Formica (✉)
Innovation Value Institute, National University of Ireland, Maynooth, Co. Kildare, Ireland
e-mail: piero.formica@gmail.com

M. Curley
Intel Labs Europe, Collinstown Business Park, Leixlip, Co. Kildare, Ireland
e-mail: martin.g.curley@intel.com

P. Formica
Master in Entrepreneurship and Technology Management, University of Tartu, Tartu, Estonia

International Entrepreneurship Academy, Via Altaseta 3, 40123 Bologna, Italy

M. Curley and P. Formica (eds.), *The Experimental Nature of New Venture Creation*,   13
Innovation, Technology, and Knowledge Management, DOI: 10.1007/978-3-319-00179-1_2,
© Springer International Publishing Switzerland 2013

taken precedence over synthesis/creation (in addition to theory always taking precedence over practice). This dissonance between the work of a university and value creation was hinted at by CK Prahalad at the 2010 Global Drucker Forum when he said, "I have never seen a next practice emerge from a regression analysis".

Increasingly, universities are moving to or are being encouraged to move to more so-called *mode 2 knowledge generation* (Gibbons et al. 1994), where knowledge is co-created in an area that is interdisciplinary, problem focussed, and context sensitive. *Mode 3 knowledge generation* "focuses on and leverages higher order learning processes and dynamics that allow for both top-down government, university, and industry policies and practices and bottom-up civil society and grassroots movements initiatives and priorities to interact and engage with each other toward a more intelligent, effective, and efficient synthesis" (Carayannis and Campbell 2012). Mode 2 and mode 3 are typically knowledge generated by collaboration with practitioners who deal with real problems in a real context, as distinct from knowledge that is generated from traditional research (called mode 1)—which is academic and based within a particular discipline (Gibbons et al. 1994).

In developments in fields such as management research the relevance problem has been highlighted (Van Aken 2005; Galavan et al. 2008). Van Aken proposed increasing the use of mode 2 knowledge production in management research in order to increase the relevance and utility of the research. Additionally, he advocated a focus on output that is field-tested and grounded.

Therefore, in these early decades of the twenty-first century a new type of university is emerging that resembles a windmill whose power is provided by the collective energy of multi-integrated players, each player corresponding to one or more blades on the windmill. This is the entrepreneurial university (Etzkowitz 2004; Andersson et al. 2010), which results in a harmonic coupling between scientific research and academic entrepreneurship. From a broader perspective, "entrepreneurship and scientific research are not in conflict after all, according to a study of university spin-outs in Italy, which found researcher-entrepreneurs are more productive than peers that are wedded to academe" (Kenward 2012; Abramo et al. 2012). The entrepreneurial university enlarges the non-conflict area between research and entrepreneurship.

Once upon a time, the monks were the forerunners of the modern university. Today, at the forefront are the corporations that, having experimented throughout the twentieth century with extensive university research outreach programs, are helping to sow the seeds for the Third Millennium of higher and advanced education with a new type of academic institution underpinned by a *university ecosystem*. Such an academic institution is an entrepreneurial University whose mission is cross-disciplinary research and education, often in the fields of convergence science[1] and technology.[2] Universities with this paradigm create a type of ecosystem

---

[1] Science: from Latin *scientia*, meaning knowledge.

[2] Examples are nanoscience and technology, digital contents convergence, intelligent convergence system. See the case of the Graduate School of Convergence Science and Technology at Seoul National University (http://gscst.snu.ac.kr/introduction/aboutus_eng.php).

that spawns technologies with the potential for exponential growth and societal transformations. Examples include the Innovation Value Institute (IVI), Intel's multi-university communities and the Singularity University.

Co-founded in 2006 by Intel and the National University of Ireland Maynooth, IVI has 75 member organizations drawn from major global corporations such as including BP, Chevron, Cisco, Fujitsu, SAP, Chevron, Ernst & Young, and Genzyme. IVI's is "to drive a structural change in the way companies and governments get value from IT" and also "to drive the transformation of management of the IT discipline through creating a global gold standard for IT professionalism". Through the use of collective and collaborative intelligence, IVI has developed an integrated set of artifacts that are beginning to be widely adopted. There is evidence of triple helix innovation (Etzkowitz 2003, 2008) at work where Industry, Government, and Academia collaborate to drive a structural improvement that exceeds what any one organization could achieve on its own.[3] IVI's funding sources include contributions from companies, universities, an Irish Government agency, and EU research funding. IVI's goal is to connect research, education, and practice in a continuous improvement loop as results and learning from field deployment of research artifacts and education programs are fed back into the research process.

In a similar broad view of new patterns of connections between Industry and Academia, Intel is striving to develop a worldwide network of university research communities, which the Santa Clara-based chip-making giant calls "multi-university communities". "Forming a multidisciplinary community of Intel, faculty and graduate student researchers from around the world will lead to fundamental breakthroughs in some of the most difficult and vexing areas of computing technology," according to Justin Rattner, Intel's CTO.[4] In the USA, Intel has created a network of Intel Science and Technologies Centres (ISTCs), while outside the USA these centers are called Intel Collaborative Research Institutes (ICRIs) Anchored at specific leading universities, a key goal is to create a research community of academics and industrialists in specific areas in order to accelerate collective progress.

---

[3] Carayannis and Campbell (2011) have proposed the concepts of Quadruple and Quintuple Helix as an extension and completion of the Triple Helix:

"The traditional Triple Helix innovation model focuses on university–industry–government relations. The Quadruple Helix innovation systems bring in the perspectives of the media-based and culture-based public as well as that of civil society. The Quintuple Helixemphasizes the natural environments of society, also for the knowledge production and innovation. Therefore, the Quadruple Helixcontextualizes the Triple Helix, and the Quintuple Helix contextualizes the Quadruple Helix. Features of the Quadruple Helixare: culture (cultures) and innovation culture (innovation cultures); the knowledge of culture and the culture of knowledge; values and lifestyles; multiculturalism, multiculture, and creativity; media; arts and arts universities; and multi-level innovation systems (local, national, global), with universities of the sciences, but also universities of the arts".

[4] http://newsroom.intel.com/community/intel_newsroom/blog/2012/05/24/intel-invests-more-than-40-million-in-worldwide-network-of-university-research-centers-to-drive-innovation.

Co-founded in 2008 by Autodesk, Cisco, Google, ePlanet Ventures, Kauffman (the Foundation of Entrepreneurship), and Nokia, the Singularity University "assembles, educates, and inspires a cadre of leaders who strive to understand and facilitate the development of exponentially-advancing technologies". Such is its popularity that in 2011 there were more than 2,200 applicants for eight graduate student slots.

The Emerging University Ecosystem

To transition from standalone research and education to integrated solutions along the knowledge value chain (from ideation to exploitation of scientific discoveries) requires universities to be reconfigured in order to construct the necessary new rules, roles, actors, and links for such a transition. It is no longer sufficient to manage in-house research and education; the university must manage an ecosystem, which is the outcome of an increasing interdependence among all partners—both internal and external to the university—that are involved in the knowledge process.

A body of knowledge, research, and education is a key part of a university. Yet, a detailed understanding of each constituent component fails to convey an understanding of the whole. The whole, which is greater than the sum of its parts, is the *University Ecosystem (UE)*—a community of personnel (professors, researchers, students, external practitioners, etc.) that interacts with one another and with other personnel from the external environment, who are pulled into its sphere of influence. The flow of knowledge is the medium that links all the personnel. In the university, knowledge is attained through study and practice, observation and experimentation. *Discovery* (the act of observing or finding something unknown) and *invention* (the process of creating a new technology), which are products of science, are turned into entrepreneurial innovation (the process of effectively bringing discovery and invention to market). This is the knowledge value chain through which the UE achieves truly meaningful success.

Box 1: The Rise of the University Ecosystems

Academic barriers are being overcome, with some universities reconfiguring their intellectual property rights policy in order to facilitate the formation of a more powerful ecosystem. For example, Penn State University no longer owns intellectual property created by industry sponsored research. "In short we consider the net present value of the interactions and relationships that our faculty and students have with industrial professionals to be real and therefore greater than the apparent future value of the proceeds from such IP," wrote Hank Foley, Penn State University's vice president for research. "Our goal … is to flatten any and all barriers or impediments to innovation and that includes our own past stance on intellectual property"

("Jumpstarting University Technology Innovation Ecosystems", Innovation Daily, April 11, 2012).

Other universities start and sustain a movement toward social networking in science or help the scientific community to bridge the gap between high-powered ideas and their beneficial impact on the market. Paul Thompson, a professor of neurology at the University of California, has highlighted the effectiveness of pooling together world expertise of more than 200 scientists in the field of brain function. "This is not usually how scientists work, and it gives us a power we have not had", said Thompson, chairman at Innovocracy—a "network of universities, colleges, innovators and supporters that connects people who want to support innovation in academic research and those innovators found on campuses around the world" (www.innovocracy.org).

In May 2012, the US National Science Foundation launched the Global Research Council, a knowledge commons ecosystem. This knowledge-based interactive global community, "which will work virtually", is designed to foster discussion on how the principles and aspirations of science might be unified across the globe. The council's first product is a set of common principles for the peer review of project proposals that will ensure that the most worthy research projects are selected".

(http://twas.ictp.it/news-in-home-page/istitutional/global-research-council-launched)

To land on the entrepreneurial planet—"the convening place for participants in today's global entrepreneurship movement", as imagined by Babson College—,the University Ecosystem (UE) needs a 'spacecraft' that harbors knowledge for a time while different stages of business development are completed: from entrepreneurial opportunity recognition to the setting up of a new venture. Science-driven entrepreneurs are the 'pilots' who convert such knowledge into innovative products and services. Their skill set is multifaced, and includes the skills of academics, scientists (the scientific entrepreneurs who start out doing university-based research) and emerging postdoctoral entrepreneurs, researchers and students, or those of leading experts from idea factories and industrial labs, R&D managers and innovation facilitators.

Search for Identity

The sustainability of a UE is determined by both its intellectual identity and its emergent culture. Its sustainability depends on the social norms and beliefs that prevail in the ecosystem. UEs oscillate between the more ordered (centralized) and the less ordered (decentralized) identity.

A centralized identity is the outcome of higher order social norms, codes, and power relations that favor the command-and-control regulation of the ecosystem. Borrowing the metaphor of (Brafman and Beckstrom 2006), we call it a "spider-like" identity. Under these circumstances, the ecosystem is configured as a centralized 'linear machine', which is set in motion by a policymaker's toolkit that encompasses regional and local clusters, science and technology parks, incubators, and other initiatives—all of which put a big emphasis on public spending. Under the jurisdiction exercised by the CEOs of those organizations and filtered through top-down bureaucracies, the emphasis is placed on the command-and-control regulation.

A decentralized identity (a "starfish" identity in the language of Brafman and Beckstrom) comes from non-hierarchically ordered social norms and spontaneous social interactions that change when new forces take action in the ecosystem. An example of such an ecosystem is the Smartbay cluster that has emerged around the Irish Marine Institute in Galway, Ireland.

In today's economic environment there are several mutating, nonlinear forces that impact adversely on the effectiveness of a linear machine model in producing a knowledge chain reaction: that is, on the process of converting the latest research outputs into new entrepreneurial ventures, which, in turn, fuel further rounds of research from their success (via both tangible and intangible resources). Today, the prevailing forces in the knowledge economy are surrounded by uncertainty, ambiguity, and ignorance about the likelihood of occurrence (if and how the new ventures grow, shrink, expire, re-emerge).

The sustainability of the UE—which is greatly affected by forces such as information asymmetry, fast-changing research and market dynamics, and barriers to research and market entry—depends on its ability to oscillate a closed and centralized approach to an open and decentralized model. This will facilitate the UE in, for example, quickly tackling the challenges or needs of the mutating forces, and back again to centralization once those forces are appeased. Therefore, a sustainable UE works according to the accordion principle; by changing its norms from those appropriate to a spider-like centralized approach to those that fit with a starfish-like decentralized model, and vice versa.

Finally, it is recognized that "Culture eats strategy for breakfast"[5]—so a crucial factor in successfully establishing a UE is visible promotion, recognition, and support for collaboration and entrepreneurship. "You get what you measure"—so universities that measure success only by the value of research funding won and the number of peer-reviewed papers published are unlikely to be successful in establishing high-performing UEs.

---

[5] "A remark attributed to Peter Drucker and popularized in 2006 by Mark Fields, president of Ford Motor Company. As the Leader of Ford, Fields was keenly aware that no matter how far reaching his vision or how brilliant his strategy, neither would be realized if not supported by the culture" (see http://www.relationaldynamicsinstitute.com/?p=48).

Trading Ideas in the Global Knowledge Economy

Business communities trade mainly in goods and services. In contrast, the trading commodity of the academic communities is ideas, and the domain in which they are traded has been transformed by a knowledge intensive globalization process that accelerates the already high mobility of ideas disembodied from goods or services. Quasi-perfect mobility moves the center of gravity of the UEs from a centralized to a decentralized identity. In a world without walls raised to protect the good ideas, UEs operate as starfish-shaped organizations that replace purely competitive mechanisms with openness and connectivity. By sharing, communicating, and renting out cutting-edge ideas to each other in a variety of forms (common research projects and papers, people-to-people and patent exchanges, cross-licensing agreements, shared copyrights, blueprints and intellectual brands), decentralized UEs are the entities that spread knowledge-intensive contents more evenly around the world and, in turn, drive the flows of global trade with ever greater speed.

Research and Entrepreneurship: A Double Trust Dilemma

To be effective, University Ecosystems (UEs) must overcome a double trust dilemma. First, *the thinkers* who generate and refine ideas for research projects and papers must trust *the doers* who bring research results to the entrepreneurial light. In turn, a stream of confidence must pass from the latter (with their ability and capacity to start knowledge-intensive businesses) to the former (with their new ideas). This virtuous circle is essential in order to facilitate the sustainability of the process in the longer term.

The categorization of thinkers and doers into specific compartments must be eliminated. From the idea generation perspective, new discoveries bring together chemists, physicists, biologists, physicians, engineers, economists, and other researchers. From an entrepreneurial perspective, innovations in business models create convergent spaces where scientific entrepreneurs and technological artisans, gradpreneurs (postgraduate/graduate entrepreneurs), enterprising graduates, and dropout entrepreneurs all work in harmony. The importance of developing an transdisciplinary environment that is instrumental to idea generation and idea implementation and exploitation cannot be overemphasized.

Experimentation Spaces

For the purpose of exploring problems and their solutions from multiple perspectives, UEs set up cross-disciplinary experimentation spaces where the interdependent partners are put together in a very free environment. On the one hand, by manipulating objects of the physical sciences, controlled experiments are conducted with the intention of pushing the scientific frontier. On the other, actions are also taken to reduce the gap between idea generation and idea exploitation, and how to mediate the conflict between the high cost of producing knowledge and the low cost of using it (Lerner and Stern 2012). As those actions that involve the complexity of human behavior fall short of the physical sciences' standard of controlled experiments, in the experimentation spaces people experience a multiplayer game of sharing ideas.

Front-runners are innovation-based growth industrial partners who leverage UEs to accelerate and amplify technologies that have been identified and investigated within the ecosystems. For example, Intel's earlier 'Lablets, were experimentation spaces that crossed different UEs where academic and Intel scientists meet. "The space allows the two groups to explore new technological fields. As soon as a marketable idea emerges it is taken out of the Lablet and potentially incubated using corporate venture funds or transferred to one of Intel's business units". Intel has no claim on the intellectual property produced by the labs, because it is interested in "helping to grow the technology and seeing where there is a usage for it within Intel" (Van Dick 2012).

Intel's Lablets were superseded in 2011 by new Intel Science and Technology Centres (ISTCs) and Intel Collaborative Research Institutes (ICRIs). ISTCs in the US and ICRIs internationally are Intel-funded, jointly-led research collaborations between Intel and the academic community. Anchored at leading universities across the globe, these collaborations form the foundations for building research communities that each focus on a specific technology area. The combination of onsite, co-located Intel, and Academic Principal Investigators with strong links to Intel Labs and Business Units increases the possibility of a stronger yield than the earlier Lablets. Intel continually strives to innovate via the process of collaborative research in order to optimize progress and output. Consequently, in the longer term, the possibility exists of establishing a dedicated research community which will mature into an ecosystem that generates value for many partners well beyond the scope of the initial community.

Conclusion: The Process of Accretion

UEs are considered accretive if they add to discoveries with a commercial potential such that they can be rapidly deployed on a large scale as a viable business. The process of accretion is enabled by the co-existence of and collision between diverse talents; in particular, two personality types: respectively, those individuals whom Nicholas Donofrio, Senior Fellow of the Ewing Marion Kauffman Foundation, has called "I"- and "T"-shaped (Donofrio 2011). The first (I-shaped personality type), which has a deep but narrow knowledge in a specialized field, is locked-in in its expertise. By combining depth with breadth across multiple disciplines, a chaotic mode is a distinguishing feature inherent to the latter (T-shaped personality type). From the "I" and "T" encounters and clashes emerge the creative expertise that pushes both knowledge and market boundaries.

The process of accretion puts on display the utilitarian facet of UEs. Study and research are not only opportunities for learning for the sake of learning—which match the classic liberal-arts model of the universities that has continued to prevail until the late twentieth century. The expertise gained through study and research is expected to lead to and forge fresh connections with the entrepreneurial experience. Contemplation and investigation are not compartmentalized and confined to the "the disinterested pursuit of truth"; instead they are intertwined with different spheres of interests that urge both faculty members and students to launch start-ups or invest in those created by peers and outsiders who revolve around their ecosystem.

Since they are open to performing any act that has the consequence of bridging the gap between intellectual ideations and commercial exploitations, members of UEs are entrepreneurial consequentialists who are central to the accretive process.

References

Abramo, G., D'Angelo, C. A., Ferretti, M., & Parmentola, A. (2012). An individual-level assessment of the relationship between spin-off activities and research performance in universities. *R&D Management, 42*(3), 225–242.

Andersson, T., Curley, G. M., & Formica, P. (2010). *Knowledge-driven entrepreneurship: The key to social and economic transformation*. New York and Berlin: Springer.

Brafman, O., & Beckstrom, R.A. (2006). *The starfish and the spider: The unstoppable power of leaderless organizations*. Portfolio:Penguin Books. England.

Carayannis, E., & Campbell, D. (2011). Open innovation diplomacy and a 21st century fractal research, education and innovation (FREIE) ecosystem: Building on the quadruple and quintuple helix innovation concepts and the 'Mode 3' knowledge production system. *Journal of the Knowledge Economy, 2*(3), 327–372.

Carayannis, E., & Campbell, D. (2012). *Mode 3 knowledge production in quadruple helix innovation systems: Twenty-first-century democracy, innovation, and entrepreneurship for development*. New York-Berlin: Springer.

Donofrio, N.M. (2011). Innovation that matters. In *Kauffman Thoughtbook 2011*. Kauffman Foundation: MO.

Etzkowitz, H. (2003). Innovation in innovation: The triple helix of university–government–industry relations. *Social Science Information, 42*(3), 293–337.

Etzkowitz, H. (2004). The evolution of the entrepreneurial university. *International Journal of Technology and Globalisation, 1*(1), 64–77.

Etzkowitz, H. (2008). *The triple helix: University–industry–government innovation in action*. New York: Routledge.

Galavan, R., Harrington, D., Kelliher, F. (2008). A work in progress. The road to relevance 15 years on—Are we there yet? EDiNEB Conference Paper, Malaga.

Gibbons, M., Limoges, C., Nowotny, H., Schwartzman, S., Scott, P., & Trow, M. (1994). *The new production of knowledge: The dynamics of science and research in contemporary societies*. London: Sage.

Kenward, M. (2012, August 19). Entrepreneurship and scientific research by academic scholars are not in conflict: Turning entrepreneurial doesn't stunt academic research output. *Innovation Daily*.

Lerner, J. & Stern, S. (2012). *The rate and direction of inventive activity revisited.* The University of Chicago Press. Chicago: ILL.

Van Aken, J. E. (2005). Management research as a design science: Articulating the research products of mode 2 knowledge production in management. *British Journal of Management, 16*(1), 19–36.

Van Dick, V. (2012). *Building and leveraging your ecosystem to spark innovation-based growth.* March/April: Ivey Business Journal.

Chapter 3
Capitalizing on Open Innovation 2.0

Martin Curley and Piero Formica

> *The more time I spent on open innovation, the more I realize it*
> *is more about mindset than a toolbox.*
> S. Balasubramanyam, Vice President, Peenya Industrial
> Association, Bangalore.

Introduction

New venture creation takes place within human–human and human–technology interactions. Experiencing interactions as they occur in the real life is in the nature of business creation. Open Innovation 2.0 (OI 2.0) is an emergent and powerful new paradigm for balancing hands-on experimentation with theoretical knowledge. In doing so, OI 2.0 provides the opportunities for elevating high ambition

M. Curley
Intel Labs Europe, Collinstown Business Park, Leixlip, Co. Kildare, Ireland
e-mail: martin.g.curley@intel.com

Technology and Business Innovation, National University of Ireland, Maynooth, Co. Kildare, Ireland

P. Formica (✉)
Innovation Value Institute, National University of Ireland, Maynooth, Kildare, Ireland
e-mail: piero.formica@gmail.com

Master in Entrepreneurship and Technology Management, University of Tartu, Tartu, Estonia

International Entrepreneurship Academy, Via Altaseta 3, 40123 Bologna, Italy

M. Curley and P. Formica (eds.), *The Experimental Nature of New Venture Creation*,
Innovation, Technology, and Knowledge Management, DOI: 10.1007/978-3-319-00179-1_3,
© Springer International Publishing Switzerland 2013

entrepreneurship through systemic changes, instead of piecemeal siloed reforms, in the experimentation process.

Globally, we are seeing increasingly more frequent and a deeper level of networking and interaction between different entities and new virtual innovation ecosystems being established. In the last century, many inventions came from the work of brilliant scientists or engineers at research facilities such as Bell Labs, IBM labs, or Xerox Parc. Over the past decade collaboration activity amongst actors in an ecosystem became more common, and this concept was conceptualized by Chesbrough (2003) as open innovation. The idea of open innovation was simple in that not all of the smart people in the world can work for your company and that ideas can pass into and out of companies.

Evolving characteristics of OI 2.0 include:

- Deeper networking including societal capital, creative commons, and communities
- A principle of shared value
- Triple to Quintuple Helix Innovation
- User involvement and user centricity
- Open flexible functional platforms for rapid evolution of solutions
- Simultaneous technical and societal innovation
- Full spectrum innovation
- Co-creation and co-experimentation
- Network effects
- Diverse ideas and divergent ideas which converge on strategic innovation vectors
- Explicit management of innovation ecosystems.

Intertwining 'Open Innovation' and 'Helices' Concepts

Chesbrough describes open innovation as consisting of five core components including Networking, Collaboration, Corporate Entrepreneurship, Proactive Intellectual Property Management, and finally a belief that R&D is crucial to the future of a company. The core philosophy underlying Chesbrough's paradigm for open innovation networking and collaboration is that innovation can be made quicker, easier, and more effective by the exchange of ideas. Chesbrough primarily sees open innovation as a way for individual companies to improve the commercialization of ideas for the benefit of the organizations involved.

Open Innovation 2.0 as defined by the EU Open Innovation and Strategy Policy group (OISPG) (Samelin et al. 2011) see the benefits of collaboration and networking from a broader perspective as a way for firms and other organizations to improve their innovation base so as to make optimal use of the societal capital and "creative commons" at their disposal. Vallat (2009) eloquently states "In addition to exchanging technology, by informal or even formal means, as in Chesbrough's ideal, the focus here is on the involvement of all actors in the innovation ecosystem, including end-users and end-user communities, brought together to share experience, information and best practices, and build strategic alliances and cross-disciplinary collaboration". This type of collaboration and networking leverages the benefits of open innovation to a fuller extent and creates a pool of capabilities, experience, and knowledge to create the so-called "creative commons". According to Vallat (2009) it favors the development of Silicon Valley Dynamics and "Positive spill-over effects stimulated by the open environment enhance value creation for the benefit of society as a whole, and not only for the firms involved".

OI 2.0 could be described as the fusion of the Henry Chesbrough's open innovation concept and Etzkowitz's Triple Helix innovation concept (Etzkowitz 2003), with extension and completion (Quadruple and Quintuple Helix) by Carayannis and Campbell (2011, 2012—see Chapter Two).

Triple Helix innovation involves Government, Academia, and Industry working together to drive structural innovation improvements beyond the scope of what any one organization can achieve on its own. Etzkowitz, the originator of the term, postulated that because this interaction is so complex it needed a triple helix rather than the double helix of DNA. In a generative knowledge economy, Industry is seen as the locus of production (product or services), governments provide a stable and defined regulatory environments as well often as investments and investment incentives while the role of Universities is changing from primarily providing a supply of trained people and education to also providing primary knowledge to the innovation process.

One example of Triple Helix innovation is Intel's network of Exascale Computing labs which have been established in France, Belgium, Germany, and Spain in conjunction with various European Universities and National Agencies to jointly perform the research which will inform the design of the Exascale computer of the future as well as understanding how best to take advantage of Exascale capabilities.

Recently, other scholars such as Carayannis and Campbell have expanded this concept to include user-led innovation and described this as a Quadruple Helix innovation process. Intel's collaborative research institutes and activities with the cities of London and Dublin explicitly comprehend user collaboration and discovery, both at design and run time, and are good examples of Quadruple Helix innovation. When diverse stakeholders align and combine creative and productive forces, everyone has the opportunity to accelerate and capture the value created.

Network Effects

Networking is at the core of open innovation and it is a socioeconomic process where people interact and share information to recognize, create, and indeed act upon business opportunities. We have all seen cases of collaboration that create effects which are at best additive, delivering a sum of the parts which is less than the sum of each of the individual components. OI 2.0 generates synergies and

Fig. 1 Synergy versus additive effects. *Source* adapted from W. M. Gore

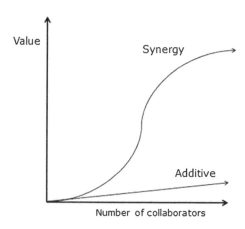

network effects rather than just additive effects. Synergy describes two or more entities interacting together to produce a combined effect greater than the sum of their separate effects. The root of the word synergy is in the Greek word "synergia" which means "working together" and this term is one way of effectively describing one key attribute of OI 2.0. A network effect is the effect that a user of a service has on the value of that service to other people, with the telephone being the classic example of the network effect. Where there is a network effect, the value of the service is dependent on the number of people using it or contributing to it. New users, players, or transactions reinforce existing activities, and there is acceleration in the number of users and value creation (Fig. 1).

Bob Metcalfe postulated Metcalfe's law and said that the value of the network was proportional to the square of the number of connected users. Reed, one of the founders of Lotus, postulated that the value of the network will come from what he calls "group-forming networks", where users come together to collaborate and generate wealth. He expressed the value arithmetically as two to the power of the number of users. As the number of users gets very large, the primary value will come from collaborative groups (Reed 2001).

The every expanding developer ecosystem that Apple established around the iPhone is a contemporary example of a network effect and many argue that this provides the greatest stickiness to the Apple products and services. Connect and Develop, the open innovation strategy pursued by Proctor and Gamble, initiated by the then CEO A. G. Laffley, is one of the most well-known examples of open innovation with Proctor and Gamble reporting that nearly 50 % of their new product ideas come from outside the company.

As networks proliferate and companies such as Intel and Cisco see pathways to connecting everybody on the planet, the opportunities to create network effects increase dramatically as the cost to connect to or contribute to a new service continues to fall and the access barriers drop. This is an unparalleled opportunity for would be entrepreneurs as access to users and computing and communications costs continue to fall significantly and a global business can be built very quickly from a bedroom or garage—e.g., Facebook and Google (Fig. 2).

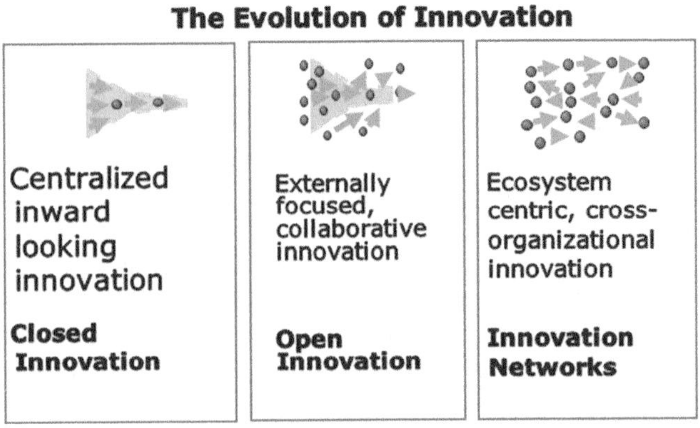

The Evolution of Innovation

Centralized inward looking innovation	**Externally focused, collaborative innovation**	**Ecosystem centric, cross-organizational innovation**
Closed Innovation	**Open Innovation**	**Innovation Networks**

Fig. 2 The evolution of innovation. *Source* B. Salmelin, DG Connect, EU Commission

Innovation Ecosystems

Innovation ecosystems can exist in many forms, in a geographic region, across a particular industry or increasingly they can be virtual not tied to a specific geography. In "Knowledge Driven Entrepreneurship" (Andersson et al. 2010) we defined a *business ecosystem as a network, or coalition, of resources, competencies, potential, energy, commitments, and promises to realize a shared profitable future.* Geographical or virtual ecosystems can span or traverse a number of business ecosystems. Bill Aulet of the MIT Entrepreneurship Centre describes seven key pods that make up the innovation ecosystems: Government, Demand, Invention/Innovation, Funding, Infrastructure, Culture and, most importantly, Entrepreneurs themselves.

Rather than letting innovation ecosystems evolve organically there is increasing recognition of the need to explicitly invest in and manage national and regional innovation ecosystems. For example to spur economic development in the state of Connecticut, Governor Dannel Malloy as part of the state's innovation ecosystem program announced four innovation hubs in October 2012 hosting financial, technical, and professional resource offerings for business. Initially costing $5 million there were funded through the Malloy's 2011 Jobs Bill. Another example is the 2010 Irish Innovation Taskforce report commissioned by the Irish Prime Minister which put developing and supporting the national innovation ecosystem at the centre of the national strategy for innovation "Building Ireland's Smart Economy".

However, innovation ecosystems are extending beyond regional and national boundaries. Hwang (2012) identified the hugely important impact of IT and networks when he wrote "Fortunately, the social networks of the future no longer need to be imprisoned by geography, as we can build overlapping social networks that traverse the boundaries of the past".

It is becoming apparent that a new more powerful kind of open innovation is happening where we have broad collaboration across many actors, with the locus of competition not only revolving around particular companies but around competing ecosystems. Consider the case of launch of Microsoft's Surface tablet which at launch was targeted to have 5,000 apps available for consumers to use. At first blush that might sound impressive, but compared to the 700,000 which were already available on the Apple iPad (see the Wall Street Journal, October 24 2012) it puts in perspective the power of a developer ecosystem surrounding a platform.

The analogy of linear momentum can be applied to innovation ecosystems with momentum being mass by velocity. The ecosystem which has the most mass (either value chain participants or users) and the highest velocity is in the strongest position to win. However, that is not always the case and small ecosystems which are agile and have high velocity can overcome the inertia of an established ecosystem. Also past success is not a guarantee of future success. Witness the struggles that Nokia/Microsoft are encountering in try to compete with the Apple iPhone and Android ecosystems.

Would-be entrepreneurs who attach themselves to fast moving ecosystems stand to derive significant benefits from the velocity of an ecosystem. We must not confuse speed and velocity. Velocity is speed x direction, and where innovations are delivered in the context of a vision vector that is much more likely to have longevity rather than ah-hoc innovations that are delivered with speed. As Stephen Covey says "begin with the end in Mind".

And yet many successful entrepreneurs did not have an end state in mind and their products or services evolved as they learnt more and collaborated with partners. With increasing interconnectivity the Internet itself creates a platform for emergence, where half-baked ideas and prototypes can be quickly piloted and iterated to deliver new value products or services. Indeed with the continuing advance of information technology, many products are becoming much more IT intensive and this creates new opportunities for technology-based entrepreneurs.

Box 1: GENIVI, An Open Source Development Platform

The mission of the GENIVI consortium is to drive the broad adoption of an open source development platform by aligning automotive original equipment manufacturers (OEMs) requirements and delivering specifications, reference implementations, and certification programs that form a consistent basis for an innovative infotainment system.

GENIVI was formed by a broad consortium of players such as BMW, JaguarLandRover, and Intel to drive efficiencies and innovation across the automotive ecosystem for so-called in-car infotainment systems.

Rather than each car company and supplier having to build custom hardware and software the goal was to develop a standard platform for infotainment that companies could then innovate on top of. The fact that many competing automotive companies and suppliers could come together successfully to collaborate to lower costs, increase agility, and accelerate

> innovations in in-car infotainment is a great example that something is fundamentally changing in the nature of innovation and collaboration.
>
> Another similar example from the computer networking industry is the Greentouch consortium led by Alcatel Lucent which is a consortium of competitors and suppliers working together around a unified mission of improving the energy efficiency of networks by a factor of one thousand from current levels.

Users, Prosumers, and Mass Collaboration

Jean Claude Burgelman identified the trend of user-led and user-centered innovation. Burgelman outlined the shift from the user as a research object to the user as a research contributor to ultimately the user as a full research participant. Intel's joint innovation lab with Nokia in Oulu where the mayor and the collective citizenry are an integral part of the innovation process is another good example of this.

Dell Computer encourages users to submit new product features and ideas to it and also allows customers vote on the top new features they would like to see in Dell products. The standout example of user-led innovation is the powerful developer community—many just individuals who contribute new apps to the Apple iPhone which transform it to a modern day digital Swiss army knife.

In parallel, the EU IT advisory group (ISTAG) identified more than a decade ago the future trend of the consumer moving to a prosumer. YouTube is an excellent contemporary example of this where users not only consume content but also create and upload content. YouTube and Facebook are forerunners of a potential much deeper level of mass collaboration that is enabled by pervasive high-speed networks and ever-increasing computing power.

The European Internet Foundation in their seminal report "the Digital World in 2025" identified mass collaboration as the emerging dominant paradigm. *Wikinomics* (Tapscott and Williams 2006) described the positive effects of peer production. The Innovation Value Institute consortium physically based in Ireland although virtually distributed across the world is an excellent example of mass collaboration amongst IT executives in which CIOs have created a model "built by CIOs, for CIOs".

With predictions of potentially, more than fifteen billion connected devices by 2015, collaboration will not be limited to increased person-to-person collaboration. There will likely be waves of machine-to-machine collaboration and person-to-machine collaborations. It is projected as the car becomes part of the network (Bill Ford announced at Mobile World Congress in 2012 that the car is now part of the network) that future cars may transmit three thousand messages per second to other cars in their vicinity. This will call for a whole new meaning of embedded computing, but will also enable mass synchronization of traffic likely resulting in earlier arrival times and more fuel efficiencies.

Additionally, an observable shift from "product" to "service" will help with the establishment of a new sustainability paradigm: A simple example of this is the adoption of cloud computing which will enable new services models which are likely more efficient and effective than each company provisioning their own hardware and infrastructure. Additionally cloud computing will also help shorten development time for new services, helping bring benefits faster to the market and to the broader society.

Shared Value

Central to the concept of OI 2.0 is the idea of shared value as espoused by Porter and Kramer (2011). Shared value is about reconceiving the intersection between society and corporate performance, seeking win–win outcomes, and being profitable through solving big problems.

Intel Corporation's vision is an example of Porter's shared value—"This decade Intel will create and extend computing technology to connect and enrich the lives of everyone on the planet". Intel believes it has both a responsibility and opportunity to connect and enrich the lives of everyone on the planet.

Porter and Kramer's idea is also an extension of C. K. Prahalad's thinking when he wrote about "the fortune at the bottom of the pyramid". Prahalad articulated a theory that companies can make significant profits by solving problems for people living in the so-called Third World. Thus the possibility exists to do noble work as well as being profitable. Ultimately this kind of thinking cannot only improve people's lives but in parallel expand collective human potential.

Ramaswami's and Guillart's book (2010) on the power of co-creation and how to boost growth, productivity, and profits nicely conceptualize a growing trend in both business and societal co-innovation. Intel Labs Europe collaboratory (co-labs) with SAP and Nokia are excellent examples of this where companies with complementary strengths, capabilities, and interests can align and accelerate innovations to the market.

Increasingly, open Flexible Functional Platforms for rapid evolution of solutions are important to provide platforms for innovation. Alexander von Gobain, Chair of the European Institute of Innovation and Technology, describes the EIT Knowledge and Innovation Communities (KIC) as "Innovation Factories" where each KIC tries to establish a distributed ecosystem to support innovation and entrepreneurship in a specific domain.

One example of an open functional innovation platform is the GE ecomagination challenge for which 3,800 ideas were submitted many by entrepreneurs with strong track records. The $200 m funding commitment by GE and four venture capital partners is a very attractive way of funding would-be entrepreneurs and the linking of similar ideas and the ability to comment on other people's ideas creates a platform for rapid emergence and evolution. The ecomagination program is another great example of share value at work representing GE's commitment to imagine and build innovative solutions to environmental challenges while driving economic growth.

The Ireland based Innovation Value Institute has developed a global platform for research and innovation in creating tools to help Chief Information officers

(CIOs) better manage their IT capabilities and improve business results through IT. Most participants in the IVI consortium both contribute knowledge and use the collective knowledge generated. Shared value is not only created through adoption of the research outputs called "artifacts", but the IVI is also catalyzing the formation of new start up consulting firms as well as helping existing consulting firms scale through provision of assessments and services.

Despite the obvious benefits of OI 2.0, is not a free-for-all where everybody can do anything and everybody has access to everything. Pisano and Verganti (2008) articulate ways to establish "which kind of collaboration is right for you" and they make a bold statement that "the new leaders in innovation will be those who figure out the best way to leverage a network of outsiders". Keys questions include how closed or open should your organizations network of collaborators be and which kind of network configuration and which problems or opportunities should the network tackle. Innovation openness is not a binary variable and at least three dimensions need to be considered (Brunswicker 2010), IP and Appropriability strategies, Innovation Search and Sources, and Relationships and networks. Pisano and Verganti (2008) describe four kinds of open innovation configurations; a closed and hierarchical network (an *elite circle*), an open and hierarchical network (an *innovation mall*), an open and flat network (an *innovation community*), and a closed and flat network (a *consortium*). Choosing which network configuration is a trade-off considering all the benefits, costs, and risks of each configuration. Importantly, Brunswicker and Vanhaverbeke (2011) identify that both a demand-driven and a widely diversified search strategy can improve the success of small and medium-sized companies in launching innovations. Thus it is vital high expectation entrepreneurs figure out how to take advantage of this new OI 2.0 paradigm.

Conclusions

In the twenty-first century mastery of and improving productivity of knowledge assets will be at least as important as mastery and improvement of physical assets and resources. EU Digital Agenda Commissioner Neelie Kroes recently said that "Data is the new gold" as she spoke about the EU open data strategy meaning that public data, generated by many administrations can become the feedstock for many new services and applications. Similarly EU Commissioner for Research, Science and Innovation Maire Geoghegan Quinn said at her EU hearing prior to her appointment that "knowledge is the crude oil of the twenty-first century" and thus our ability in Europe to leverage the collective intelligence of the entire community can create great opportunities in our future knowledge society.

Doblin's Keeley has articulated an innovation taxonomy he calls the 10 types of innovation (Keeley et al. 2013), and this particular model has helped break down the linear science to innovation model which pervaded much policy making and public funded research. There is increasing recognition that innovation goes well beyond the scope of just technological invention and that innovation is a socially complex process where multifaceted actors (organizations, individuals, universities, governments etc.,) interact to create products and services which create value and are adopted.

Keeley identified business model innovation, networking or ecosystem management, and customer experience as key areas of high innovation return on investment and increasingly researchers have to think holistically how their research might ultimately make a market impact. EU Commissioner Geoghegan Quinn coined the phrase "from research to retail" to help extend researchers thinking to how their contributions might benefit society further than just through knowledge generation (important though that is).

Open Innovation 2.0 involves specifically designing national or regional innovation ecosystems. The European Innovation scorecard identifies input, intermediate, and output indicators of national research ecosystems. A key goal is to design autocatalytic clusters. Rifkin (2011) explores how Internet technology and renewable energy are merging to create a powerful "Third Industrial Revolution". He asks us to imagine hundreds of millions of people producing their own green energy in their homes, offices, and factories, and sharing it with each other in an "energy internet," just like we now create and share information online. This would be another form of OI 2.0.

Digital Innovation is being driven by the intersection of Moore's law and the explosion of mobile wireless communications. The continuing exponential growth in computing and communications power and bandwidth, respectively, are creating all sorts of new possibilities and each year new things which were previously seen as difficult to achieve or near impossible are being routinely achieved. In effect, Moore's law is colliding with virtually every domain creating disruption and new exciting value adding possibilities. In parallel, we see much business and societal innovation to take advantage of digital innovation and this means that the most impactful digital innovations will be those which have both usefulness and ease of use attributes.

As we look forward, we believe that three important trends are converging which will help create a better future:

- accelerated digital transformations
- mass collaboration and
- a new paradigm of sustainability.

The confluence of these three trends can help improve quality of life, enable an innovation economy, and move us all toward a more sustainable trajectory for our societies and economies. Developments such as the imminent introduction of electric vehicles in Europe which will require a whole new infrastructure is an example of where digital transformations, mass collaboration, and sustainability are coming together.

We often think the hard part of innovation is the creation of the idea but very often innovation diffusion and adoption are much harder. Having so many more people connected also enables them to participate in the innovation process enabling so-called collaborative intelligence. Marketing like many disciplines is being revolutionized by digital technologies. One of the key advantages is the possibility of personalized marketing while also experimenting in real-time and adjusting marketing programs in real-time based on feedback. Perhaps, the biggest opportunity is to involve the end-user or customer in the innovation process while better discovering their wants and needs while also engaging them in the innovation process itself.

Globally, we need to emphasize high expectation entrepreneurship as a mechanism for stimulating jobs and sustainable growth. As we show in the next chapter, high expectation entrepreneurship occurs when an emerging disruptive technology collides with high ambition and is especially important as according to the Global Entrepreneurship Monitor high expectation entrepreneurs contribute up to eighty percent of all jobs. Knowledge-based service industries are especially suitable as candidates for high expectation entrepreneurship.

All in all, the combination of the emerging OI 2.0 coupled with high expectation entrepreneurship creates an unparalleled opportunity for making progress.

References

Andersson, T., Curley, G.M., and Formica, P. (2010). *Knowledge-Driven Entrepreneurship: The key to social and economic transformation*. New York and Berlin: Springer

Brunswicker, S. (2010), "Open Innovation", Presentation at Innovation Value Institute Summer Summit, Maynooth Ireland.

Brunswicker, S., & Vanhaverbeke, W. (2011). *Beyond open innovation in large enterprises: How do Small and Medium-Sized Enterprises (SMEs) Open Up to External Innovation Sources?* Available at SSRN: http://ssrn.com/abstract=1925185.

Carayannis, E., & Campbell, D. (2011). Open innovation diplomacy and a 21st century fractal research, education and innovation (FREIE) ecosystem: Building on the quadruple and quintuple helix innovation concepts and the 'mode 3' knowledge production system. *Journal of the Knowledge Economy, 2*(3), 327–372.

Carayannis, E., & Campbell, D. (2012). *Mode 3 knowledge production in quadruple helix innovation systems: Twenty-first-century democracy, innovation, and entrepreneurship for development*. New York: Springer.

Chesbrough, H. W. (2003). *Open innovation: The new imperative for creating and profiting from technology* (p. xxiv). Boston: Harvard Business School Press.

Etzkowitz, H. (2003). Innovation in innovation, the triple helix of university-government-industry relations. *Social Science Information, 42*(3), 293–337.

Hwang, V. W. (2012). What's the big deal about innovation ecosystems? *Forbes* 7/10.

Keeley, L., Nagii, B., & Walters, H. (2013). *Ten types of innovation: The discipline of building breakthroughs*. New York: Wiley.

Pisano, G., & Verganti, R. (2008, December). Which kind of collaboration is right for you. *Harvard Business Review*.

Porter, M. E., & Kramer, M. R. (2011, January). Creating shared value. *Harvard Business Review*.

Ramaswamy, V., & Guillart, F. (2010). *The power of co-creation: Build it with them to boost growth, productivity, and profits*. New York: Free Press.

Reed, D. P. (2001, February). The law of the pack. *Harvard Business Review*.

Rifkin, J. (2011). *The third industrial revolution: How lateral power is transforming energy, the economy, and the world*. New York: Palgrave MacMillan.

Samelin, B., Curley, M., Honka, A., Sadowska, A., & OISPG (2011). *Service innovation yearbook*. Luxembourg: EU Publications.

Tapscott, D., & Williams, A. D. (2006). *Wikinomics: How mass collaboration changes everything*. New York: Portfolio.

Vallat, J. (2009), *Intellectual property and legal issues in open innovation in services*. Brussels: EU OISPG Publication.

Chapter 4
Laboratory Experiments as a Tool in the Empirical Economic Analysis of High-Expectation Entrepreneurship

Martin Curley and Piero Formica

> *There is no such thing as a failed experiment, only experiments with unexpected outcomes.*
> Richard Buckminster Fuller, American engineer and architect, 1895–1983

> *It doesn't matter how beautiful your theory is, it doesn't matter how smart you are. If doesn't agree with experiment, it's wrong.*
> Richard Feynman, American theoretical physicist, 1918–1988

M. Curley (✉)
Intel Lab, National University of Ireland, Collinstown Business Park, Leixlip, Co. Kildare, Ireland
e-mail: martin.g.curley@intel.com

Technology and Business Innovation, National University of Ireland, Collinstown Business Park, Leixlip, Co. Kildare, Ireland

Innovation Value Institute, National University of Ireland, Collinstown Business Park, Leixlip, Co. Kildare, Ireland

P. Formica
Innovation Value Institute, National University of Ireland, Maynooth, Co. Kildare, Ireland
e-mail: piero.formica@gmail.com

Master in Entrepreneurship and Technology Management, University of Tartu, Tartu, Estonia

International Entrepreneurship Academy, Via Altaseta 3, 40123 Bologna, Italy

M. Curley and P. Formica (eds.), *The Experimental Nature of New Venture Creation*,
Innovation, Technology, and Knowledge Management, DOI: 10.1007/978-3-319-00179-1_4,
© Springer International Publishing Switzerland 2013

Introduction

When technology advancements meet entrepreneurship, market novelties are created over time and turned into high-expectation —firms launched by 'high-expectation' entrepreneurs with the intention of growing them significantly (Box 1). These firms pursue the commercialization of innovative new processes, products, or services. That encounter between new technology and the entrepreneur is a force that pushes the economy away from a state of equilibrium. In fact, high-expectation entrepreneurship provokes disequilibrium, a state of change-induced imbalance with no tendency to stasis. In this sense, high expectation entrepreneurship is high-impact entrepreneurship—the kind that drives the growth of technology industries and one of the factors that shape the economy into an open, complex and adaptive system.

High-expectation entrepreneurship deserves special attention because of its substantial impact on economic growth. According to the Global Entrepreneurship Monitor, fewer than 7 % of nascent entrepreneurs expect to employ 50 or more employees within five years; however, the economic impact of high-expectation entrepreneurs is disproportionately positive as they account for up to 80 % of the total expected jobs created by all entrepreneurs.

Box 1: Technology Meets Ambition: Ryanair

An outstanding example of the growth that can occur when technology advancement meets entrepreneurship is that of Ryanair. At one point a small struggling Irish regional airline, its oversized ambition began to be realized when a business innovation it copied from Southwest Airlines intersected with the emergence of the Internet and Internet reservations systems which dramatically reduced the transaction and distribution costs associated with passenger reservations. In this case Ryanair was able to adopt the tried and trusted model of Southwest Airlines—point-to-point flying, coupled with a single aircraft type fleet to minimize the total cost of ownership while flying into smaller regional airports with lower landing charges.

While this model was successful, Ryanair had been limited by the degree to which it could scale its own call center to handle the expansion of its business. The arrival of the Internet and Internet reservation systems

---

enabled the company to scale new routes and improve yields quickly through a ubiquitous Internet interface and computer-based yield management systems. As Ryanair introduced new routes, passengers had immediate and easy access to low fares, and a network-type effect was created. Almost overnight Ryanair was seen as a transformative force in European airspace, creating not just a medium for low-cost holidays but also and more importantly a platform for enabling entrepreneurship in Europe as the travel costs associated with business meetings became much more affordable, thus enabling new physical connections and meetings to take place, creating in turn new options and enabling new business.

These kinds of physical interaction could not have taken place in the previous prohibitively high fare environment. The fact that at one point Ryanair's market capitalization surpassed the total value of Lufthansa and British Airways combined shows the power of high-expectation entrepreneurship. It is important to note that, prior to the success of Ryanair, multiple different business model experiments had been tried which burned real capital.

The presence of an experimental laboratory environment, which could simulate different business models taking into account consumer behavior, regulatory changes and other environmental factors, could help similar high-expectation entrepreneurial activity to reduce expenditure and accelerate the path to profitability.

Furthermore, and to give an example for a group of highly developed countries, a 1 % increase in the general rate of entrepreneurial activity raises economic growth by 0.11 %, while a 1 % increase in high-growth entrepreneurship has a $2\times$ multiplier effect, yielding a 0.29 % increase in GDP growth (Stam et al. 2007).

High-expectation, high-impact entrepreneurs (Box 2) exhibit high ambitions that produce unpredictable growth patterns: from exponential and oscillating to declining and collapsing trends. As long as these entrepreneurs inject energy into the economy, which derives from the flow of information and human interaction involved in the creation of new ventures with high expectations, the system remains open to all possible states: sometimes it is near equilibrium or in an equilibrium-like state, while at other times it may exhibit a state very far from equilibrium.

In addition, an entrepreneurial venture's potential to induce disequilibrium can lead to a variety of management responses, which may be under-restrained, over-restrained, or critically restrained due to the uncertainty and probable high velocity of the venture. Moreover, complexity and adaptation emerge as significant characteristics of the economic system insofar as all agents involved in the creative process of high-expectation new ventures interact and adapt to each other and to the context in which they find themselves embedded.

Purposeful, high-expectation entrepreneurs explore with new eyes the uncharted territories of unforeseen circumstances and undiscovered opportunities. This approach contrasts with the expansion of existing business, in which much is known already about the business and many of the assumptions are based in fact, derived from available data. Entrepreneurs, on the other hand, grow new markets from scratch, and their creations are evolutionary organisms with a propensity for innovation (Box 3). The solutions they devise for complex problems can be empirically validated in laboratory-style experiments in which the function and performance of high-expectation start-ups are evaluated. The results of such experiments give entrepreneurs, financiers, and policy makers a deeper understanding of the actual workings of real-world new markets.

Box 2: Characteristics of High-Expectation, High-Impact Entrepreneurs
High-Expectation

High-expectation entrepreneurs account for just 7 % of global start-up activity. However, they make a disproportionately large contribution to economic prosperity and job creation. The high-expectation entrepreneur is typically a young male, has a higher education qualification, comes from an upper-income household, and has little fear of failure. According to a report from an international audit and advisory organization:

1. Education and household income, as well as entrepreneurial activities and attitudes, were significantly associated with high-expectation and high-growth entrepreneurship. High expectation and high-growth entrepreneurs had a higher level of education than other entrepreneurs and the general population.
2. Only 30 % of all categories of entrepreneurs were women, whereas less than 25 % of the high-expectation and high entrepreneurs were female.
3. An individual's decision to launch a new venture is affected by both the environment and his or her personal characteristics and skills. "It's a combination of these two elements that determines whether a particular opportunity has potential for growth in the eyes of any potential entrepreneur," said Hilton Saven, senior partner of Mazars Moores Rowland, the South African arm of the Mazars group.
4. There is a sharp division between early stage, high-expectation entrepreneurs and their already established high-growth counterparts. Almost 20 % of the early-stage group were between 18 and 24-years old, while only 3 % of the established group fell into this age bracket, with more than 50 % over 45-years old.'

Source Report released by the accounting and advisory group Mazars in collaboration with the Global Entrepreneurship Monitor. The report was based on interviews with 678,714 adults spanning 53 countries over 6 years, making it the largest study of high-growth entrepreneurship yet conducted. It provides important clues as to the make-up of the high-expectation entrepreneur. Quoted from Sanchia Temkin, 'Entrepreneurs "not solution to unemployment"', *Business Day—News Worth Networking*, 16 August 2008.

High-Impact

Age

Start their companies when they are between 26 and 45-years old

Education

More likely than entrepreneurs from lower growth companies and the general population to have college or graduate degrees

Mindset

Work in partnerships

Little fear of failure

Conduct a significant portion of their business internationally

Once become successful, they are the most likely to start funding other ventures as angel investors.

Growth

>20 % per annum is the estimated growth rate of their firms

Expect to add between 3 and 15 times more jobs than low-growth businesses

Source Ernst & Young, Global Entrepreneurship Monitor and Endeavor, *2011 High-impact entrepreneurship global report.*

The report is based on a survey of more than 800,000 people in 60 countries worldwide of whom over 70,000 were entrepreneurs.

Box 3: Innovation

Innovation is the tool of the entrepreneur (Drucker 1993). Innovation is the introduction of something new which creates value for the organization that adopts it (Baldwin and Curley 2007). Experimentation for the entrepreneur will often focus on adoption of the innovation and the value that is created for both the end consumer and the entrepreneur and the potential ecosystem that is required to deliver the innovation. For an innovation to be sustainable it has to deliver value to the end consumer, the entrepreneur and the innovation and delivery ecosystem; otherwise the life of the innovation and the associated entrepreneurial activity will be short.

The laboratory experiments show how high-expectation entrepreneurs should cultivate market outcomes, which behavior should guide trust building between the founders and their potential investors, and how policy makers should design and test the 'rules of the game'. Persistent beta states for the business model and underpinning venture offerings become the norm. Rapid experiment iteration and rapid solution prototyping go hand-in-hand for the high-expectation entrepreneur, with plateaus of stability introduced into the iteration cycle to enable commercialization and the capturing of value from the evolving offerings.

In the educational context, high-expectation entrepreneurship could be cultivated by drawing on the experiences of medical schools, where different performance learning modes have been created and have become an integral part of educational and research activities. In particular, a business school should go beyond detached diagnoses and develop proper experiments, even experiments that are therapeutic in nature, and test ideas clinically in interaction with private and public organizations.

In Ireland, the Irish Management Institute has established a business laboratories program to support this kind of experimentation, focused on broader organizational challenges. IMI BizLabs operates as a business think-tank which brings together active communities of interest in the area of organizational challenges. It works through:

- solution-driven research addressing current business challenges;
- industry-led collaboration with organizations to codesign solutions; and
- ongoing research team investigation.

Experiments, Simulations and Clinical Treatments

Experiments

Defined as 'managerial behavior which consistently exploits opportunities to deliver results beyond one's own capabilities' (Thompson 1999, p. 209), entrepreneurship requires enterprising individuals who can identify new opportunities and implement them accordingly. Thus entrepreneurship is a skill, learned through experience, and improved with practice. With experience as the centerpiece for entrepreneurial development, the probability that entrepreneurs will learn from their experiences greatly increases.

Entrepreneurs continuously accumulate experience by conducting and evaluating experiments in the marketplace. Before their entry into the market process, for inventing and innovating would-be entrepreneurs economic experimentation labs offer new locus for experimental activity. Experiences gained in such labs produce a range of perspectives to help the decision maker limit his or her exposure to risk and uncertainty when it becomes time to carry out experiments in the marketplace.

Laboratory experiments test propositions derived from the idea spectrum (Fig. 1). On the basis of experience, new business ideas need to be processed

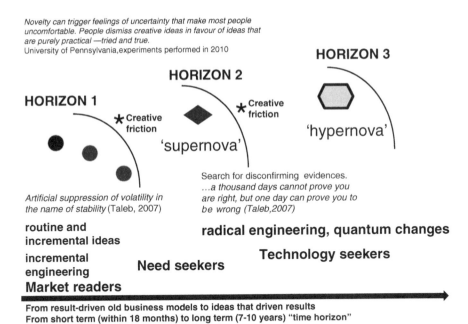

Novelty can trigger feelings of uncertainty that make most people uncomfortable. People dismiss creative ideas in favour of ideas that are purely practical —tried and true.
University of Pennsylvania,experiments performed in 2010

HORIZON 3

HORIZON 2

HORIZON 1

★ Creative friction

★ Creative friction

★ Creative friction

'hypernova'

'supernova'

Artificial suppression of volatility in the name of stability (Taleb, 2007)

Search for disconfirming evidences.
...a thousand days cannot prove you are right, but one day can prove you to be wrong (Taleb,2007)

routine and incremental ideas

radical engineering, quantum changes

incremental engineering

Need seekers

Technology seekers

Market readers

From result-driven old business models to ideas that driven results
From short term (within 18 months) to long term (7-10 years) "time horizon"

Fig. 1 The idea spectrum: what drives the innovation impulse

through the monitoring and revising of their underlying assumptions and of the performance/reward predictions embedded in those assumptions.

Figure 1 Decription

Shifting from one horizon to the next, creative frictions generate new entrepreneurship. "Friction of rivalling principles increases the rate of mutation", which means: redefinition, redeployment, and recombination of resources" (Stark 2009).

Quantum changes mostly come from high ambitious entrepreneurs outside established businesses, engaged in an endless succession of experiments.

Within Horizon 1, we find "I"-shaped individuals whose expertise is profound, 'one mile deep', but the range of vision is 'one centimetre width'. Those who head to Horizons 2 and 3 are "T"-shaped individuals—those who add to a deep expertise a wide range of knowledge and interests. They instigate learning across disciplinary boundaries.

"Apple's edge, says Prof Verganti [Polytechnic of Milano], stems from Steve Jobs' experience in the entertainment industry. As the founder of Pixar, when he returned to Apple in 1996 he came at the music, movie and gaming industries as an insider. By being able to interpret the world beyond computers, he could arrange the puzzle of content and technology more successfully than many" (http://philipdelvesbroughton.com/2010/11/03/).

"I"-shaped experts at Technogym-The Wellness Company create "mainframe hardware" exercise equipments. "T"-shaped experts at Nintendo recreate, thanks to Wii—a home video game console, Technogym "on your waist".

'**Supernova**': An idea explosion that is more energetic in terms of entrepreneurial potential than a standard 'nova'.

'**Hypernova**': Which has energy substantially higher than a 'supernova'.

"**Market readers**": Pursue their customers more cautiously, preferring to innovate incrementally and keeping a close eye on the innovations of competitors.

"Like need seekers, they must pay careful attention at the ideation stage to what customers are looking for in the products they choose—but in their case, the goal is to make sure they are delivering successfully differentiated alternatives.

"Market Readers also seek to track the technology trends that can help them create that differentiation".

"**Need seekers**": Ascertain the needs and desires of consumers and then to develop products that address those needs and get them to market before the competition does.

"The capabilities required for success begin at the ideation stage, where need seekers pursue open innovation and directly generated, deep consumer and customer insights and analytics, as well as a detailed understanding of emerging technologies and trends, in order to identify both their customers' needs and the technology trends that can help them meet those needs".

"**Technology drivers** begin with a different approach to ideation, using their technological prowess to develop products their customers may not know they need".

Source Barry Jaruzelski and Kevin Dehof, *The Global Innovation 1,000: How the top Innovators Keep Winning*, Booz & Co., 17 May 2011

Moving along the entire spectrum is an exercise that has the double hump nature of the learning curve. Once crossed a given horizon, the experimenter realize that things are more complicated than she/he thought. Therefore, the experimenter has to return to fundamentals to think through alternative opportunities. Iteration, the act of repeating the experimental process, is an innate trait of the entrepreneurial experimentation.

In laboratories participants learn the language of the market by:

- conducting a test or investigation;
- direct observation of events (Box 4);
- social interaction with their peers; and
- experiencing realistic conditions that imitate or estimate how events might occur in a real company, in the industry in question, in the marketplace, and so on.

Box 4: Events in process

New product/service ideas are events in process which call for a particular set of abilities to reduce the high level of risk intrinsic in the process from creativity to implementation of the business idea.

Laboratories performing experiments on business ideas put in motion a chain of events. Examples of events in process are:

- The business idea is absorbed as a nutrient into the body of the founding entrepreneurial team. Then it is disseminated among the team members.
- Knowledge prior to action is closely and dialectically interwoven with actions deemed appropriate to ascertain information about the business idea under investigation.

> Consumers' preferences, which are unpredictable and subject to continuous transformation (Hayek 1944), are submitted to a process of discovery—imperfect as it is, for perfect rational decisions are often not feasible in practice (Simon 1957).

Learning from experience and implementing the experimental results are two essential steps that high-expectation entrepreneurs should consider to reduce the level of risk intrinsic in new ventures focused on innovation.

Experimental results indicate what policies can be developed to reduce the start-up time significantly. The less the time needed to complete the launch of a new venture, the lower the start-up costs, the less up-front capital required and the higher the probability of the venture actually getting started. Moreover, experimental results point to strategies that will be conducive to interaction between established firms and experimental ventures. Through such interaction, a new venture can benefit from the accumulated experience of the existing companies in terms of accelerated innovation and growth (Fig. 2).

Equally relevant is the re-evaluation effect. On the basis of experience, the conclusion may be reached that an experimental business has to change direction. Such experiment-induced behavior, if pursued by high expectation entrepreneurs who see lab experiments as a potential stimulant for the evolution of their business, constitutes a source of advantage over established firms, which tend to attribute bad results to underperforming managers rather than to mistaken predictions.

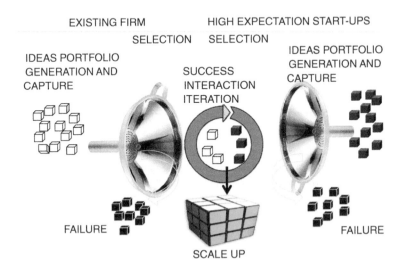

Fig. 2 Two sides of experimentation: established firms and experimental ventures (*Source* adapted from BCG analysis (Reeves et al. 2010))

Last but not least, since pattern recognition is an inherent feature of human nature, laboratory experiments can provide ambitious entrepreneurial individuals seeking fast-growing business opportunities with a chance to assess ideas and strategies, and learn how to achieve pattern completion. Thus those who underperform because of difficulties in the process from pattern recognition to pattern completion can obtain help from business lab clinics.

Simulations

Simulations use mathematical or physical models to reproduce the conditions of a situation or process. Business simulators situate players in a virtual situation in which they have to make decisions. Simulations push them not only to think, but also to understand how the real business world works, what they should keep in mind and how their decisions affect the performance of a whole company (Box 5).

Box 5: Objectives of Simulations

- To interpret correctly real-world (simulated) situations and to train participants to make and quantify decisions.
- To make participants familiar with the creation of new ventures and all the aspects of that process.
- To carry out a critical analysis of complex business inter-relationships.
- To enable participants to manage growth and organizational change.
- To clarify the consequences of decisions taken.
- To train participants in how to draw up and systematically use objectives to run a company.
- To improve participants' strategic thinking, linking strategies to objectives, and then linking those objectives with decisions.
- To improve teamwork and organization.

The simulation process is an interactive learning method, in which the goal is to learn business by doing business in a risk-free environment. The learning player will have to make decisions to start-up and run his or her company according to different simulation stages: from the actual marketplace relevant to the business idea, so that the simulation can run according to 'reliable' data (on competitors, market share, sale of similar products, average pricing, alternative products, etc.), to the generation of random data through which to discover unpredicted events or scenarios in a way that is close to reality. It is important to note that simulators, as learning tools, increase performance, enhance the development of business and entrepreneurial skills, and reduce the costs of making errors in real life. A correct interpretation of the results can provide useful feedback to players so that they can adjust their efforts to master the subject matter. More than winning, the objective is to learn how to behave in certain circumstances—that is the real value of playing a 'smart game'.

Clinical Treatments

If experimental and simulation approaches try to avoid dangerous and expensive errors once the start-up is engaged in the real-world market, the clinical approach is designed to address problems encountered either during lab experiments or in reality. In this sense, it plays a role equivalent to that of the therapeutic counsellor who tries to cure a client's disease. Clinical treatments shift patients from a state of passivity and low expectation to a state of activity and high expectation, encouraging them to challenge what they are told by business experts, to seek second opinions and collect information proactively.

Entrepreneurial Experimentation

By 'entrepreneurial experimentation' we mean a method that relates a business concept to an experiment. The idea is that the concept creator is then stimulated to build on the concept in the light of the laboratory experimentation. Since the opportunity cost of experimentation decreases with the increase in value of a new business venture, high-expectation entrepreneurs, whose high-value-added business propositions bear low opportunity costs, are likely to show greater propensity to conduct experiments than are entrepreneurs who are pursuing low-value added activities.

Would-be entrepreneurs start with beliefs and ideas that they want to turn into a business. By running experiments, business ideas move from an embryonic state to full manifestation in the form of new ventures. In particular, conducting experiments gives potential entrepreneurs with high expectations an opportunity to learn how to mobilize their new ideas to anticipate change, take a chance on the future and structure their business in such a way that it can gain access to the marketplace quickly and successfully.

The quantitative and qualitative data collected during experimental (and clinical) exercises make it easier for entrepreneurs to ask for support from financiers, to evaluate the pros and cons of pure financial backers versus strategic partners, to seek industrial allies, and to recruit employees. Anyone familiar with high expectation start-ups knows that the key to success is access to experienced people who can bring both talent and funding to the new venture.

Exposure Modes

Would-be entrepreneurs may be exposed to modes of experimentation which are either analogical or conjectural. The analogical mode accomplishes the task of shrinking the potential entrepreneur's area of known ignorance about her or his business idea. Analogy-based reasoning can be applied to the known unknowns of a new concept whose business domain has attributes in common with those of another domain. The analogical method is represented by the typical case-based approach: past cases from a different domain are used to highlight possible solutions for problems incurred with the new idea.

The conjectural mode proceeds by trial (involving the spontaneous, serendipitous discovery of building blocks for the business idea under experimental scrutiny) and error (leading to the elimination of elements that are demonstrated to be inappropriate). High-expectation business concepts sail into uncharted waters, exhibiting unfamiliar traits of novelty and complexity. The entrepreneur, who is unaware of her or his ignorance, is thus exposed to a voyage into unknown unknowns. High-expectation propositions, therefore, cannot be treated by analogical reasoning and, specifically, case-based reasoning. When no apparent rules or commonalties can be applied, trial-and-error is the approach that can support an imaginative and conjecture-based process of discovery. The major cost of this approach is the time invested in yielding a solution from the iterative process, triggered by selecting what ex ante looks like the most suitable choice set. If something does not work, the process has to be iterated until an appropriate answer is found.

Experiments in Collaboration

Agent-Based Experiments for International Start-Ups

Experiments in collaboration involve people who are keen to communicate across their knowledge boundaries. The main objects of such collaboration are macroeconomic and social changes, such as those brought about by the creation of international start-ups.

Until recently global business was thought to be the exclusive domain of large multinational corporations and business conglomerates. It is increasingly recognized, however, that entrepreneurial firms have a crucial role to play in international business (Mtigwe 2006). Indeed, the steady proliferation of internationalization has led to the inevitable development of entrepreneurship without borders (Formica 2005). Experiments in collaboration in this particular context, in which new ventures are exposed to international tensions and pressures, can serve as a prologue to micro-experiments focusing on a specific venture opportunity.

One kind of collaborative experiment on the nature and perspective of international start-ups has been carried out at the University of Tartu in Estonia. In

2006–2007 would-be founders of new firms participated in the university's Master's class in Entrepreneurship. Teams of three to five students, all engaged in the content and context business processes of new venture creation, were at the heart of a collaborative experiment to test cultural values, psychological behavior, and business approaches to international start-ups. Through the experimental session, the Master's students underwent a process of self-examination and were thus encouraged to make a conscious effort to adopt an open mindset in their approach to new venture creation.

The Tartu experiment made it clear that the ability to manage and capitalize on international start-ups posed numerous challenges. Some start-ups whose founders are embedded in different countries and cultures will be successful, but many may fail: a critical factor is that the knowledge required to flourish will not be found in textbooks, but rather in the budding entrepreneur's fellow classmates halfway across the globe.

Participants in the Tartu experiment pinpointed internal and external environmental conditions (Figs. 3, 4) that were conducive to cross-border start-ups. Encompassing decision making, customer service, distribution, and communication, the internal environment of internationally founded firms seemed promising for the students. The greater creativity and innovation on offer, along with a better understanding of local values and customer demands, meant for them that the advantages largely outweighed the disadvantages. Concern did emerge, however, regarding delays in decision making and delivery, along with miscommunication between employees.

As for the external environment, the participants easily identified the political and legal advantages of internationally founded firms. Other economic factors, such as currency volatility, were less readily noted. Concerns were expressed about the difficulties of integrating the legal and political characteristics of each individual country and of dealing with cultural clashes among employees. These difficult factors, however, were considered to be outweighed by reassuring aspects, such as the increased access to technology and access to foreign currency hedging that would be available.

Fig. 3 Internal environmental conditions conducive to international start-ups

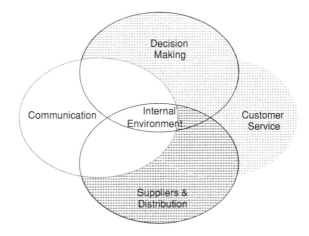

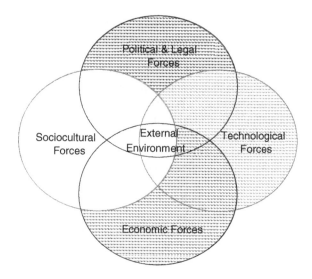

Figure 5 shows a mind-map summarizing the overall results of this collaborative experiment conducted at the University of Tartu in pursuit of actions conducive to new venture creation by means of international start-ups.

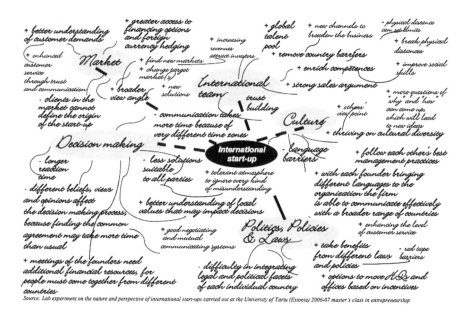

Source: Lab experiment on the nature and perspective of international start-ups carried out at the University of Tartu (Estonia) 2006-07 master's class in entrepreneurship

Fig. 5 Mind-map by would-be company founders on the nature and perspective of international
start-ups

'Periodic Table' of Experimental Elements

An experimental lab, in which business concepts are processed, can be seen as a kaleidoscope of experimental elements. Each experiment consists of *n* elements, which are organized in groups. We have identified five element groups: inputs, process, actions, outputs, and impact.

The five groups and their elements (of which we have identified 18) are displayed in a 'periodic table' of experimental elements. In Fig. 6 those elements belonging to the same group are arranged in a vertical line. The proximity of a given element to another depends on the intensity of their reciprocal interaction and influence. The higher the interaction and influence, the closer they are. Since economic experiments compete with one another, and each experiment is unique and cannot be replicated, for a given starting condition—that is, a given business concept—no deterministic law can be drawn as to the placement of elements in the periodic table. Notwithstanding, with experiment after experiment an adequate cumulative experience can be accrued, resulting in probabilistic predictions of a given element's relative intensity in terms of interaction and influence.

The layout of Fig. 6 is just one example of how experimental elements interact and affect one another. The horizontal lines, or 'periods', show two different experiments triggered by two different business concepts. Figure 6 can be refined and extended over time as new elements are identified, new groups are created and new predictive models are developed to explain the entrepreneurial behavior over a given business concept process.

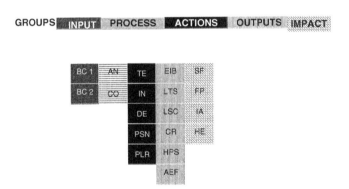

Fig. 6 'Periodic table' of experimental elements (*BC* business concept, *AN* analogical, *CO* conjectural, *TE* test, *IN* investigation, *DE* direct observation of events, *PSN* participation in social networks, *PLR* placing the learner under realistic conditions, *EIB* experiment-induced behavior, *LTS* less time to complete a start-up launch, *LSC* low start-up costs, *CR* much less upfront capital required, *HPS* higher probability of new start-ups getting underway, *AEF* source of advantage over established firms, which tend to attribute bad results to poor management as opposed to mistaken predictions, *SF* support from financiers, *FP* evaluate financial backers versus strategic partners, *IA* seek industrial partners, *HE* hire employees)

Conclusions

In this chapter we have introduced and emphasized the relevance and importance of high-expectation entrepreneurship as a driver of economic growth. Entrepreneurial ventures differ dramatically, from extensions to existing businesses to high-expectation start-ups in which little is known and much has to be assumed. Using a translational innovation approach, paradigms borrowed from both experimental research and the practice of medicine have been adopted as vectors for accelerating the experimentation and validation of business models associated with high-expectation entrepreneurship.

The ability to transpose, test and iterate new business ideas and models in a laboratory environment has significant potential. When coupled with approaches such as Discovery Driven Planning (McGrath and MacMillan 1995), emerging software platforms that can simulate markets and consumer reactions, or help predict demand for new products, can lead to rapid learning, iteration and the preliminary validation of a new business idea—thus mitigating risk, avoiding potential cost, and maximizing potential revenue.

References

Stam, E., Suddle, K., Hessels, S., Jolanda, A., & van Stel, A. J. (2007). *High growth entrepreneurs, public policies and economic growth*. Jena Economic Research Paper, No 2007-019, School of Business and Economics, Jena: Friedrich-Schiller University.

Drucker, P. (1993). *Innovation and entrepreneurship*. New York: Collins.

Baldwin, E., & Curley, M. (2007). *Managing IT innovation for business value*. Santa Clara: Intel Press.

Thompson, J. (1999). The world of the entrepreneur: A new perspective. *Journal of Workplace Learning, 11*(6), 209–224.

Stark, D. (2009). *The sense of dissonance: Accounts of worth in economic life*. Princeton: Princeton University Press.

Hayek, F. A. (1944). *The road to serfdom* (ARK edn, 1986). London: Routledge and Kegan Paul.

Simon, H. (1957). A behavioral model of rational choice. In *Models of man, social and rational: Mathematical essays on rational human behavior in a social setting*. New York: Wiley.

Reeves, M., Sahla, H., & Bokkering, M. (2010). *Simulation advantage*. Boston: BCG Perspectives.

Mtigwe, B. (2006). Theoretical milestones in international business: The journey to international entrepreneurship theory. *Journal of International Entrepreneurship, 4*(1), 5–26.

Formica, P. (2005). The argument for international entrepreneurship in the knowledge economy. In *Structural change in Europe 4: Entrepreneurial spirit in cities and regions*, Bollschweil: Hagbarth.

McGrath, R. G. & MacMillan, I. (1995). Discovery driven planning. *Harvard Business Review, 73*(4), 44–54.

Chapter 5
Accelerating Venture Creation and Building on Mutual Strengths in Experimental Business Labs

Martin Curley and Piero Formica

The common measure of all value is man.
Abbé Ferdinando Galiani, Della Moneta, 1751.

Introduction

The time is ripe for a new and far-reaching approach to the idea production process and, particularly, the idea testing process of high-expectation entrepreneurial ventures. The consolidated approach of science and technology incubators, which has its roots and rationale in the industrial era, is supposedly based on the

M. Curley · P. Formica (✉)
Innovation Value Institute, National University of Ireland, Maynooth, Co. Kildare, Ireland
e-mail: piero.formica@gmail.com

M. Curley
Intel Lab, Collinstown Business Park, Leixlip, Co. Kildare, Ireland
e-mail: martin.g.curley@intel.com

Technology and Business Innovation, National University of Ireland, Maynooth, Co. Kildare, Ireland

P. Formica
Master in Entrepreneurship and Technology Management, University of Tartu, Tartu, Estonia

International Entrepreneurship Academy, Via Altaseta 3, 40123 Bologna, Italy

M. Curley and P. Formica (eds.), *The Experimental Nature of New Venture Creation*,
Innovation, Technology, and Knowledge Management, DOI: 10.1007/978-3-319-00179-1_5,
© Springer International Publishing Switzerland 2013

subsidized protection of aspiring entrepreneurs. However, high-expectation entrepreneurs typically move much more quickly than supporting agencies, and therefore for them the reality is different from the theory. As reported on August 8 2012 by broadstuff, the weblog of multi-media consultancy Broadsight—www.broadsight.com, findings from a study by Jared Konczal of the Kaufmann Foundation "reveal that the effects of incubation are potentially deleterious to the long-term survival and performance of new ventures. Incubated firms outperform their peers in terms of employment and sales growth but fail sooner".

Increasingly, in the knowledge era, companies have adopted or are now ready to embrace creativity-driven and productivity-driven open models of innovation. In this new climate, business initiators can help to raise the productivity of their founding teams by earlier exposure to the benefits and indeed the risks of open innovation. This is why we propose an experimental laboratory approach, in which young minds with an aptitude for new venture creation can be opened up and energized through intelligent exposure to risk (Apgar 2006).

Entrepreneurship-Redefining Markets

The boundaries of future entrepreneurship may be redefined by a cluster of innovations that will shock the current entrepreneurial fabric. Clean-technology entrepreneurial ventures will create an environment in which clean-energy technologies (such as electrified vehicles, carbon capture and storage, and concentrated solar power) can be adopted and spread. The transformation through technological innovations of the auto and utilities sectors will encourage new entrepreneurs to kick-start electrified vehicle businesses (including battery producers, communications and infrastructure providers and electric car manufacturers) to leapfrog over the current mainstream competitors (Woetzel 2009; Hensley et al. 2009) through disruptive innovative action (Christensen 1997).

Entrepreneurship-redefining markets will also stem from developments such as green affordable housing; health 2.0 (that is, improving healthcare delivery through ICT support, offering the prospect of sharing experiences and best practice to enhance the focus of development efforts[1]); genetic engineering; nanotechnologies; and the fusion of nano, IT and genetic sciences.

---

[1] The International Organization for Knowledge Economy and Enterprise Development (IKED), a think-tank based in Malmö, has designed and implemented the Patient Certificate Scheme (PCS) "to enable people to become more aware, and to be empowered, so as to take the measures needed to counter pressing health issues and thus promote long-term wellness, whether proactively or when a disease has already struck". The PCS has established a network of partners around the world, including think-tanks, universities and private as well as public agents engaged in health services and communication.

Made possible by the evolution of new Web technologies (and indeed of low-cost airlines such as Ryanair and AirBerlin), which make human interactions more valuable and less costly, collaborative networks have been developed to enhance the intensity and impact of entrepreneurial activity that is promoted and demanded by innovation-based economics. In an experimental business laboratory, where innovative business ideas with high-growth expectations can be tested, a network of interconnections binds aspiring entrepreneurs, experts and non-experts together in unlikely ways, with the non-experts challenging the biases of the expert and instigating learning across disciplinary boundaries. Such an environment provides a key opportunity for the radical transformation of the business-as-usual habit, as each participant learns from the experiences of the other participants. The result is a 'hyper-entrepreneurial', turbocharged, innovation-friendly business culture.

The 'Possibility' Approach

In their book Knowledge-Driven Entrepreneurship: the Key to Social and Economic Transformation, Andersson et al. (2010) portray the experimental business lab as a network of outsiders (various entrepreneurial individuals 'federated' from universities, research labs, start-ups and business partners), each facing the formidable task of becoming part of an innovation ecosystem rather than relying on himself herself. The resulting interactions begin to produce social and economic factors which promote an entrepreneurial cohesion that in turn will lead to the formation of the innovation ecosystem.

In well-established experimental labs, what matters goes beyond an evidence-based approach, founded on data from inside and outside the laboratory, to a 'possibility' approach (Box 1). In Einstein's words, 'the intuitive mind is a gift from God and the logical mind is a faithful servant': entrepreneurs need to demonstrate both approaches. Key elements of the experimental laboratory strategy are, first, to test the bounds of possibility ('ideation') and, second, to gather information on the bounds of probability (diffusion and business model testing). New ideas with the potential to create value can fail to do so because of problems of adoption (Baldwin and Curley 2007): an experimental laboratory offers the key value-added opportunity of testing potential adoption or diffusion paths before significant capital has been spent.

Next, to help aspiring entrepreneurs test their hypotheses, the business lab must recognize the presence of unseen processes. The behaviour and actions of individuals in the lab system have key implications for the aspiring entrepreneurs. The aspiring entrepreneurs can perform experiments along a spectrum from the known knowable to the unknown unknowns. They can include complex, chaotic issues and cover a vast range of other factors, such as morale, self-motivation, a 'naive optimism' bias, tolerance to risk, trust, concern for fairness, and herding behaviour and other human tendencies in contemporary economic life.

By inquiring into unseen processes, experimental labs attempt to shape a community of entrepreneurs whose members complement each other's strengths. No participant perceives a threat from the strength of the others and each perceives a stake in the others' success. This is the classic 'win–win' situation, reflecting an 'abundance mentality' (Covey 1989) which accepts that knowledge multiplies when it is shared (Amidon et al. 2005; Andersson et al. 2010).

Box 1: The Possibility Approach in the Context of Experimental Laboratories

Qualitative in nature, the possibility approach is 'a means of assessing to what extent the occurrence of an event is possible and to what extent we are certain of its occurrence, without, however, knowing the evaluation of the probability of this occurrence. This can happen, for instance, when there is no similar event to be referred to' (School of Rural and Surveying Engineering, National Technological University of Athens, www.survey.ntua.gr/main/labs/rsens).

An experimental business laboratory should include the four elements that constitute the concept of possibility:

- 'permission' (aspiring entrepreneurs are allowed to process their business ideas);
- 'feasibility' (it is possible to process business ideas);
- 'plausibility' and 'consistency' (judging the possibility of occurrences, bearing in mind their compatibility with available knowledge and experience).

The business idea is thus treated as an assumption or a conjecture, based on incomplete information and imprecise or vague knowledge.

The possibility approach, which deals with uncertainties, guides the investigation of the business idea within the experimental laboratory.

From Social to Value Networks

Social networking has great appeal for aspiring entrepreneurs, who see in social gathering places (both physical and virtual) the preconditions for co-creating content, products and services. In this respect, the work of experimental labs is to turn socially-driven relationships into value-led network interactions that increase the possibility of radically enlarging the scope and reducing the cost of trying out a business idea with high-growth expectations.

Whereas social networks are concerned with connecting people, value networks dig deeply into the who (who the participants are), where (where they come from/where they are going), why (why they are in the network), and how (how they interact). We may summarize the nature and significance of value-led networks in the context of experimental business labs as follows:

- Since 'value is a relationship between people' (Ferdinando Galiani, Italian economist, 1728–1787), connectivity is the focus. People with different backgrounds and expertise are connected so that they can test their business ideas by working together. An individual's choices are thus intertwined with the choices of others ('social influence').
- Network relationships are visible to all parties and are guided by performance. The lab's 'temperature' is taken by applying mathematical rigour to the assessment of how personal interactions are affecting the lab's entrepreneurial community. Network mathematics quantifies how connected the members of a lab are.
- The idea evaluation process assigns a degree of compatibility to a given idea in terms of its relevance to and connection with the network.
- The network learns through exposure to various situations. Signals are transmitted from one business idea to another.
- Patterns of business ideas are discovered. This makes it possible to move across adjacent market boundaries. Permutations and combinations of business ideas are possible (Fig. 1).

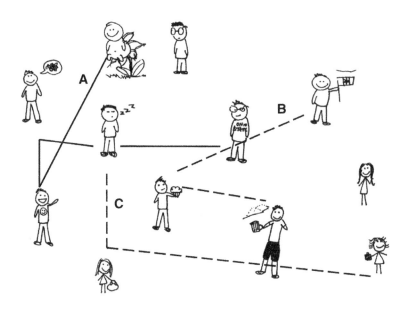

Fig. 1 Peer-to-peer dynamics in an experimental lab community

In the collaborative economy of experimental laboratories for new venture creation, knowledge-to-business achievement teams constitute a collective, networked intelligence of knowledge-driven individuals with an entrepreneurial mindset. Each of them is an "atomic component" of the lab community, which is "built on a great number of pairs of atoms" (Hwang and Horowitt 2012). They can extend their knowledge to recognize innovative business opportunities where others do not, to prove the power of their business concepts, and to stretch out their capabilities by forging their relationships with other peers. Experiments also highlight how vitally important the 'rules of the game', laws, regulations, customs, truth, and honesty are in determining both individual behaviour and market outcomes.

Peer-to-peer dynamics releases a considerable amount of energy needed to transform innovative business ideas into successful ventures.

The experimental lab community is a platform where business ideas are being posted looking for problem seekers and problem solvers (Montana and Charnov 2000). The first actively seek out and attempt to deal with problems as they arise from the community ideas. The latter identify effective solutions by enabling "unobvious connections" of different ideas (Piller 2010) Teams of problem seekers and problem solvers are interchangeable. Today's "problem A" team seeker is tomorrow's "problem B" team solver.

Laboratory participants experiment combination and permutation and business ideas through the exploration of adjacent connections. The lab creates an environment where information can spill over from project A to projects B and C. Interactions are apparently boring until there is a collision.

'Medici Effect'

An experimental lab is, therefore, both a physical and a logical environment which enables and facilitates two key stages of the innovation and entrepreneurial process: the creation of an idea and the early testing of possible diffusion patterns to determine its potential viability and its probability of success.

From a creativity point of view, the experimental lab creates a kind of super-collider environment in which a 'Medici effect' can occur (Johansson 2004), with breakthrough ideas and insights emerging at the intersection of different disciplines, cultures and entrepreneurial individuals. As we move forward, it is likely that the information intensity of new products and services will continue to increase and that the Internet of the future will emerge as the dominant delivery channel for them, especially for the services.

Arguably, the future shape of the Internet, with improved quality of services, guaranteed service-level agreements, and improved mobile access through technologies such as WiMax, will enable a Cambrian-like explosion of new knowledge or, indeed, the kind of new Renaissance envisaged in a report on the European Research Area (EU 2009).

Applying Osterwalder's (2004) taxonomy of business models, an environment supported by a computing platform could be created which would enable the rapid simulation of product and service innovations, and the associated business models, to enable early learning about market potential and profitability prospects without significant cost. The integration of the Bass Diffusion equation (Bass 1969) and other diffusion theories into a simulation environment (Rogers 2003; Moore 1991) would enhance the simulation and contingency testing.

Such an environment would lower the entry barriers to entrepreneurship by making a rich context for experimentation available to the aspiring entrepreneur. The development of such a virtual environment will require a high degree of focus, but is in itself a market opportunity for an aspiring high-expectation entrepreneur. Market prediction techniques that enable more accurate forecasting of demand for new products using gaming theory are already showing significant promise (Erhun et al. 2007). The use of multi-player, multi-media virtual environments to conduct experiments and learning in the context of homeland security is also indicative of the promise of such approaches.

Conclusions

The lessons learned from the Great Recession and the Euro crisis call for a new global socio-economic model. Experimental labs will help entrepreneurs to learn not only about value, but also about values.

C. K. Prahalad (Wartzman 2009) argues for a world in which business is an instrument of social justice. According to Drucker (1973), the purpose of business should not just be to make profit: businesses should understand that profit is the outcome of doing the right things in the right way. Perhaps aspiring entrepreneurs in experimental labs can incubate and demonstrate the kind of leadership the world will surely need.

References

Andersson, T., Curley, G. M., & Formica, P. (2010). *Knowledge-Driven Entrepreneurship: the Key to Social and Economic Transformation*. Springer: New York and Berlin.

Apgar, D. (2006). *Risk intelligence: Learning to manage what we don't know*. Boston, MA: Harvard Business School Press.

Baldwin, E., & Curley, M. (2007). *Managing IT innovation for business value*. Santa Clara: Intel Press.

Bass, F. (1969). A new product growth model for consumer durables. *Management Science, 15(5)*, 215–227.

Christensen, C. (1997). *The Innovator's Dilemma*. Boston, MA: Harvard Business School Press.

Drucker, P. (1973). *Management: Tasks, Responsibilities, Practices*. New York: Harper & Row.

Erhun, F., Gonçalves P., & Hopman, J. (2007). The art of managing new product transitions. *MIT Sloan Management Review*.

EU (2009). *Preparing Europe for a new renaissance: A strategic review of the European research area*. Brussels: European Commission.

Hensley, R., Knupfer, S., & Pinner, D. (2009). Electrifying cars: How three industries will evolve. *McKinsey Quarterly*.

Hwang V. W., & Horowitt, G. (2012). *The Rainforest*. The Secret to Building the Next Silicon Valley, California,USA: Regenwald, Los Altos Hills.

Johansson, F. (2006). *The medici effect: Breakthrough insights at the intersection of ideas, concepts, and cultures*. Boston, MA: Harvard Business School Press.

Montana, P. J., & Charnov, B. H. (2000). *Management* (3rd ed.). New York: Barron's Educational Series.

Moore, G. (1991). *Crossing the chasm: Marketing and selling products to mainstream customers*. New York: Harper Business.

Osterwalder, A. (2004). The business model ontology – a proposition in a design science approach. *PhD thesis, HEC Lausanne*.

Piller, F. T. (2010). From market places to problem places: report of the quebec seeks solutions conference—A new method for open innovation. Mass Customization and Open Innovation News, A Blog by Frank T. Piller, December 17, 2000, http://mass-customization.blogs.com/mass_customization_open_i/2010/12/from-market-places-to-problem-places-report-of-the-quebec-seeks-solutions-conference-a-new-method-fo.html

Rogers, E.M. (2003). *Diffusion of Innovations* (5th ed.). New York: The Free Press.

Wartzman, R. (2009). Authentic engagement, truly. *Business Week*, 4 December. http://www.businessweek.com.

Woetzel, J. (2009). *China and the US: the potential of a clean-tech partnership*. McKinsey Quarterly, August.

Chapter 6
From Entrepreneurial Fission to Entrepreneurial Fusion: Achieving Interaction Resonance in a Micro-Innovation Ecology

Martin Curley, Piero Formica and Vincenzo Nicolò

> *... innovations do not arrive fully fledged but are nurtured through an experimentation process that takes place in laboratories and development organizations.*
>
> Stefan H. Thomke, 2003

M. Curley · P. Formica
Technology and Business Innovation, National University of Ireland, Maynooth, Ireland
e-mail: piero.formica@gmail.com

M. Curley
Innovation Value Institute, National University of Ireland, Maynooth, Kildare, Ireland
e-mail: martin.g.curley@intel.com

Intel Labs Europe, Collinstown Business Park, Leixlip, Kildare, Ireland

P. Formica (✉)
Master in Entrepreneurship and Technology Management, University of Tartu, Tartu, Estonia
e-mail: piero.formica@gmail.com

International Entrepreneurship Academy, Via Altaseta 3, 40123 Bologna, Italy

V. Nicolò
Freelance advisor in the area of Industrial R&D, Bologna, Italy
e-mail: vin.nicolo@gmail.com

President of the Technical Board of the Italian Machine Tool Builders association, UCIMU, Milano, Italy

Via Guglielmo Marconi 41, 40122 Bologna, Italy

M. Curley and P. Formica (eds.), *The Experimental Nature of New Venture Creation*,
Innovation, Technology, and Knowledge Management, DOI: 10.1007/978-3-319-00179-1_6,
© Springer International Publishing Switzerland 2013

Introduction

There is a growing pressure on the business incubator community to design real-world experiments and act on the basis of a systematic body of evidence which goes beyond the conventional territory of the business plan where teams of aspiring start-up founders operate in isolation of one another to project cash flows that have a little basis in reality or diverge so far from or it as to be unusable.

As agents of change, company founders lack perfect knowledge and information about future events. Think of what could happen by jumping from one S-curve[1] to the next. If guided by a business plan model that is consistent with the rational expectations hypothesis,[2] those agents performing that jump see a 'mathematical' coincidence between their expectations and the business plan's predictions (statistical expected values). Considering all errors to be random, the new scenario from the business plan is plausible and the act of jumping promises to enact innovation effectively.

The unpredictable elements in the future (i.e., in the new S-curve) are too great to be captured by rational expectations—namely, consistent business plan models. In this respect, business plans look like a static collection of facts (i.e., 'known unknowns', 'things that don't move'—Taleb 2007), the predictability of which succumbs to unexpected events (the 'black swan' in Taleb's terminology) that may occur in the uncertain and dynamic environment. Therefore, an entrepreneurial process of effective innovate implies the recognition and acceptance of a culture of how to handle uncertain expectations. Stepping outside the boundaries demarcated by rational expectations is the challenge entrepreneurial agents of change have to face. The effectiveness of innovation is dependent on its execution, which occurs via the innovation agent's ability to navigate the incertitude of the future.

The new context for starting and growing innovative firms shifts the focus on the business process development, defined as a set of potential entrepreneurs and novel ideas randomly assigned to different teams, and approached as a series of experiments. Each team is an experimental unit to which treatments are administered. Each treatment is unique in terms of identification, clarity, and variability of the questions of interest that the experiment is intended to answer. The number of experimental units, the power of interbreeding them, and the number of treatments running in parallel create the conditions for a thorough exploration of novelty-driven entrepreneurial opportunities.

---

[1] The S-Curve illustrates the introduction, growth, and maturation of innovations as well as the technological cycles that most industries experience.

[2] ``Rational expectations are the hypothesis in economics which states that agents' predictions of the future value of economically relevant variables are not systematically wrong in that all errors are random" (Wikipedia: Rational expectations). As Skidelsky (2009, pp. 33–36), biographer of John Maynard Keynes, says, "By means of rational expectations…..economists came to believe that the future was certain…..In the history of thought, rational expectation hypothesis represents a fusion of the rational aspirations of the Enlightenment with that belief in the 'wisdom of the crowd' characteristic of American democracy".

A series of iterative experiments turn business assumptions into facts which mitigate risk taking. Since there are not reliable statistics of entrepreneurial expectancy, we assume that risks in the process of a new venture creation are not probabilistically measurable. Risk mitigation is the outcome of facts that convey the message of entrepreneurial uncertainty and, therefore, do not ignore the messiness of reality, the cumbersome presence of 'unknown unknowns' and the possibility of extreme events. Business plan models that project in the future previously observed patterns do not capture experimenters. They use the data of experience that reflect significant changes in a world of uncertainty and imperfect information.

"Idea building" is the first in the series of experimentation. Experimenters test a rudimentary business idea, although it is not conducive to a successful new venture. This flash of inspiration has the advantage of creating a language that moves the experiment forward, thanks to the formulation of a strategy and the interaction with other teams. At the end of this stage, a prototype shall be available.

"Idea reformulation or re-evaluation" is a second set of experiments. Experimenters get from a few potential customers feedback through which the original business concept with its assumptions could be reformulated or re-evaluated.

"High growth potential" is featured in the third stage of experimentation, which the experimenters manage with the intention of building a bridge between the very small base of early-bird customers and the wide platform of pragmatic buyers.

Entrepreneurial Fission and Entrepreneurial Fusion

Incubators have a substantial history of consolidated practice which involves breaking down the potential start-up business into its component parts and then providing support services accordingly to each part. Thus, an incubator might respond to an aspiring entrepreneur's demand for information and assistance (I&A) by providing consultancy services (through a cohort of intermediaries) to assess and improve the entrepreneur's ability to draft a business plan, in order to start the new business; and by providing office premises and related business support services. This process, which, to use the language of nuclear physics, we define as 'entrepreneurial fission', is regulated by a (subsidized) price mechanism as far as the demand for and supply of I&A is concerned (Box 1).

Despite early optimism, entrepreneurial fission has not fulfilled expectations. Often, the 'energy' that a prospective venture could generate is inhibited by the self-contained work of the specific component parts—separated and isolated from the start-up process, and each possessing a lighter 'nucleus' which has defined modes of interaction with the other nuclei. These interactions do not serve a specific business idea: the focus is not on identifying and removing the uncertainties of the particular business idea through a rapid learning process, but rather on making the new business fit a formalized view of what a business should look like. The reason why this happens lies in the very nature of the incubator. In the traditional incubation process, information and assistance provided to a start-up culminates in the business plan whose static nature and predictability collide with the dynamic environment, outside the incubator, where the plan needs to be executed.

Box 1: Incubators are not a quick fix

'For years incubators or entrepreneurship centers that provide financial help, mentoring, and often space to start-ups have been popular with governments. But I have seen scant rigorous evidence that these expensive programs contribute commensurately to entrepreneurship. One municipality in Latin America established 30 small incubators, but after several years only one venture out of more than 500 assisted by them had reached annual sales of $1 million. Though Israel's renowned incubator program has helped launch more than 1,300 new ventures, relatively few of them have been big entrepreneurial successes. On the basis of my discussions with Israeli officials, I estimate that, among the hundreds of Israeli ventures that have been acquired at hefty valuations or taken public, at best 5 % were hatched in incubators. And incubators definitely are not a quick fix. When well conceived and well managed, they can take 20 years or longer to generate a measurable impact on entrepreneurship. Poorly conceived and managed, they can be white elephants.'

Source Isenberg (2010)

In contrast, the experimental business laboratory, a new type of high-expectation start-up accelerator, shifts the focal point from lighter nuclei, which shape the demand for and supply of I&A in writing a business plan, to a combination of the various components of the start-up process. In essence, this involves the setting up of a micro-innovation ecology (Goldstein et al. 2010), in which generative leadership can occur and the nexus of relationships is the major source of influence, the driver of innovation and, indeed, the regulator of change. This approach creates a fusion of the demand for and supply of knowledge and experience (K&E)—that is, the experiential knowledge (having experience) and experiential learning (gaining experience) that occur as the new business prepares to set sail into the uncharted waters of 'unknown unknowns', 'things that move', 'unexpected events', and 'black swans' (Fig. 1; Taleb 2007).

We give this process the name 'entrepreneurial fusion', in which, to use the nuclear physics metaphor, multiple nuclei join together to form a single heavier (more intimately connected) nucleus. Unlike the price-led coordination of demand for and supply of I&A in the context of an incubator, where consultants are remote from and external to the entrepreneurial teams, the experimental lab combines different personality types, high-expectation aspiring entrepreneurs included, into an experimental team (the heavier nucleus). 'Active experimenters', as we call them, run the experimentation process as an integrated whole. They partake in a symbiotic relationship with one another, built on a solid foundation of trust. This results in a form of interaction resonance (Goldstein et al. 2010) which leads to novelty experiments that are at the core of innovation.

The relationship patterns are characterized by a hybrid of evolutionary mentoring and coaching (Table 1) and these patterns are dynamic and fluid, according to changing needs that arise during the process of experimentation. In these business labs the focus is on finding the shortest path to gaining experience with the as-yet unknown aspects of creating a business out of a new idea. Relationship ties, based on shared vision and objectives, replace the price mechanism as the glue that holds everything together.

An innovation ecology or ecosystem will survive and thrive only when the exchanges of ideas, energy, and resources among participants are vigorous, plentiful, and sustainable (Goldstein et al. 2010). This means that the design, environment, and governance of an experimental lab are critically important, with required generative leadership as well as bottom-up interactions are vital for the achievement of 'nuclear fusion'.

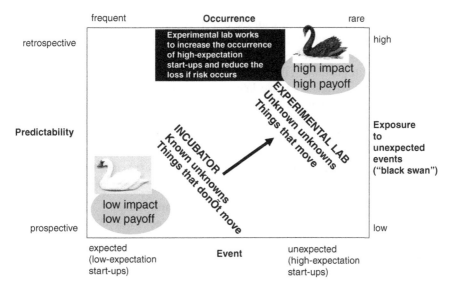

Fig. 1 From incubatorincubator to experimental lab: From ordinary to extraordinary. *Source* adapted from Taleb 2007

Table 1 From functionalist to evolutionary mentoring and coaching

Functionalist	Evolutionary
Mentor: facilitate, question, listen	*Mentor*: challenge, build, inspire
Coach: instruct, direct, teach	*Coach*: engagement with transformation
Focused on:	Focused on:
Enhancing performance	Exploring potential
Improving an existing skill or	Changing direction
developing a new one	Breaking new ground

Source adapted from Pasieka (2010) and Brockbank and McGill (2006)

Active Experimenters

To try, rather than to analyse, is the priority for active experimenters. While 'paralysis by analysis' is a very common syndrome resulting from the practice we have characterized as entrepreneurial fission,[3] experimental labs—by definition—encourage a culture of experimentation[4] and offer aspiring entrepreneurs the freedom to create their own subject matter—to study, experiment with and change it, to succeed or, in the case of failure, to fail fast and save time (Fishback 2009).

Whereas analysis is often based on consolidated knowledge, in new businesses, as in a game of Mastermind, the knowledge of the past combination of pins is of little help.[5] In the game, in order to find the winning new combination it is necessary to carry out trials and learn from the errors made. The focus therefore shifts from the overemphasized process of analysis to the undervalued process of synthesis which, in this context, is the combination of ideas and materials (intangible or tangible) into an integrated value proposition, business model, and operating plan, with the result that the initial idea is provided with the direction and scale of a path to successful growth and is able to withstand the demands of ever-changing environments.

A design for experimental practice has to be developed to eliminate critical uncertainties as early as possible in the process. With an attitude similar to that of Thomas Edison, active experimenters make laborious, careful, and experienced attempts to validate a new or different start-up idea which contains some 'active principles' that derive from faithful assumptions. In this light, they do not consider an experiment that fails as a failure: a failed experiment is seen as an indirect step to success—even to an achievement that may substantially exceed what was expected—through a process of discovery revealing that a particular method does not work (Sloane 2010) (Box 2).

Box 2: Experimentation encompasses success and failure
Active experimenters find out what does and does not work through an iterative process—that is, through a repeated cycle of successive approximations of what works, what does not work, what has to be changed and what requires further testing.

---

[3] Service intermediaries are normally paid with time-based fees and not in accordance with the results derived from their operations. Time-consuming analysis leads to higher fees.

[4] As Reeves et al. (2010) observed, adopting a culture of experimentation means that companies "appreciate the necessity of an experimental approach, embrace creative dissatisfaction with the status quo, provides incentives that encourage experimentation and remove barriers that discourage it, measure the effectiveness and economics of experimentation rigorously, tolerate failure as a necessary part of learning, soften internal and external boundaries to facilitate collaboration, cultivate statistically literacy and a hunger for information".

[5] In this context, the reference to Mastermind relates to a board game Mastermind (rather than the BBC television quiz game of the same name) in which one player, the code breaker, seeks to decode a pattern of colored pegs set by the other player, the code maker. A feature of the game is that the code maker provides feedback to the code breaker as the latter suggests an answer, so that the code breaker can learn from incorrect guesses, as the game unfolds.

Active experimenters do not delay experiments because they may result in failure. Early failure can lead to greater success faster. When experiences about accumulated failures are shared and can be used for subsequent investigations, others in the experimental business lab's network have an opportunity to learn lessons from the failures and even to find successful ideas for new ventures from them. Thus experiments that do not work as expected are not seen as failed experiments which put the lab's community at a disadvantage.

The adoption of agile software methods facilitates both the earlier discovery of how to build a successful software product or service, and, more importantly, the faster discovery of user requirements and the product/service functionality or features that will appeal to users. In a manner similar to that of the automotive industry using 'concept cars' to convey future designs and obtain feedback, this process can be used to discover more rapidly what is desired or needed by users of a future product or service. In looking to the market, experimenters can create prototype solutions that meet a current or future need, or invent something that creates a desire for a 'discretionary' product or service.

Active experimenters look beyond their own limits of expertise in order to collaborate across disciplines and sectors. Performing experiments on business ideas is an exercise in observing events, questioning premises, associating seemingly unrelated concepts and problems from different fields, and engaging with a rich variety of individuals (Dyer et al. 2009) from diverse cultural, ethnic, linguistic, and religious backgrounds. This is the type of creative process relentlessly undertaken by active experimenters, the innovative idea holders, with their teams, peers, and experienced mentors and coaches, as well as non-experts who challenge any overconfidence, overreaction, and other behavioral biases the experts may exhibit.

These participants all cope with significant complexity because they are engaged in experiments that consist of many different but connected parts. However, good experimenters are cautious and are alert to the dangers of complications that may make things more difficult or more confusing. Together, the experimenters shape an ecosystem in which ideas move from insight and inspiration to implementation and in which the outstanding ones are converted into successful business ventures.

The effect of a shared laboratory is to enhance the propensity of the lab's population to become entrepreneurial. Immersed in the culture of experimental labs, active experimenters trigger multidirectional flows of information, knowledge, and productive discussions, all of which involve the entire spectrum of business ideas 'housed' in the lab. This means that active experimenters construct cross-business, interactive experiences that can provoke unexpected and unconventional responses to the implementation of initial creative insights and inspirations. Thus, creativity truly occurs if and when the entrepreneurial team acts in concert with the surrounding population of experimenters. This is a characteristic of the phenomenon of 'emergence' (Goldstein et al. 2010) or, in other words, the coming into being of new business ideas, models, and products/services. In innovation ecology, emergence is the basis for innovation—the key issue is how an ecology of innovation can generate unique experiments that will yield insights leading to business or socially entrepreneurial ideas with high potential.

However, creativity and ideas are not innovation; they are only constituent parts of it. To make innovation happen, the entrepreneurial team and its collaborative pool of experimenters must show an ability to:

- test false hypotheses obtained by incomplete analysis;
- perceive mistakes as opportunities to learn rather than risks;
- prove the relevance and viability of the business concept by creating prototypes and submitting it to a target audience of potential users who can see, use, or evaluate the team's innovation; and, finally,
- launch a business with sufficient finance and a robust business model.

Experiment-Related Decision Processes

Entrepreneurial decision processes are the decision-making processes undertaken by active experimenters with regard to the implementation of a potential business. Two critical issues they must address are the type of innovation and the business growth rate.

Innovation can be directional or intersectional (Johansson 2006); and a decision process can be focused on delivering slow or rapid growth. In turn, the pace of growth can be consistent or inconsistent with regard to the type of innovation enacted.

Directional Versus Intersectional Innovation

As described above, individuals acting in different fields, disciplines, and cultures are the experimental team players. This unique structural characteristic makes an experimental team inherently predisposed to the cross-exploration of a business idea. Cross-exploration activities test the value of the idea through a combination of different concepts: the combination may be 'usual' or 'unusual'. In the latter case, fields, disciplines, and cultures normally considered to be unrelated to one another are brought together—and thus the experimental team demonstrates that the idea under investigation constitutes an intersectional innovation: ultimately, it could launch a totally new industry. On the other hand, if the outcome of the experiment is a 'usual' combination, this indicates that the idea has the potential to further the development of an existing industry in a pre-established direction. The business idea thus constitutes a directional innovation (Johansson 2006).

Slow Versus Rapid Growth

Experiment-related entrepreneurial decision processes need to resolve difficult questions. The following is an illustrative list. These questions apply to high-expectation start-ups, the main target of business lab experiments.

- Is explosive growth synonymous with high ambitions for growth?
- The trajectory to success has the shape of a pair of scissors, of which the two blades are, respectively, low and rapid growth rates: which trajectory maximizes the chance for success, and under what circumstances?
- Alternatively, is there a third way that is more viable for modulating the business pace of an ambitious idea?
- What balance needs to be struck by the bearer of the ambitious idea who, like the two-faced Roman god Janus, must look two ways—in one direction toward a massive, unexpected event that could generate stratospheric growth, and in the other direction at the need to build a business solid enough to grow smoothly over time?
- How can the high exposure to unexpected events be controlled without endangering the high impact and high pay-off a high-expectation start-up seeks?

Consistency Between Innovation and Growth Patterns

The experimental team is called on to prove that the innovation and growth patterns underlying the business idea are acting in concert. Major discrepancies between the two will threaten both the reliability and the stability of the evolutionary process that moves the business idea from concept to implementation in the real world.

Experimental control, which discriminates factors producing a clear 'signal' from the 'noise' or other disturbing elements, eventually leads the experimental team to consider alternative plans that may give higher confidence of success. This should help avoid a scenario in which a start-up fails because of an unwillingness to deviate from the original plan.

Conclusions

The concept of nuclear fusion we have expounded in this chapter is also useful as a metaphor for the type of businesses that must be launched in the future. As with fusion, in which there are high releases of energy with potentially less toxic waste produced than from nuclear fission, the world needs new kinds of businesses that optimize not only cost and market efficiency and effectiveness but also ecological (Wuthrich 1999) and resource efficiency.

In the future we shall need a new socio-economic model that emphasizes qualitative development instead of qualitative growth. Growth is more of the same stuff, while development is the creation of better stuff with lower resource intensity (Daly 2008). It is increasingly argued that we are reaching the limits to growth and that we need to evolve into a steady-state economy (Daly 2008), with a significant focus on the dematerialization of products and their accompanying supply chains.

Creating an experimental business lab with the overall design constraint that all the innovations emerging from it must demonstrate improved resource efficiency could act as a lighthouse project, building awareness, and catalyzing other approaches to the development of sustainable innovations which contribute to qualitative development and progress.

References

Brockbank, A., & McGill, I. (2006). *Facilitating reflective learning through mentoring and coaching*. London: Kogan Page.

Daly, H. E. (2008). *A Steady State Economy—a failed growth economy and a steady-state economy are not the same thing; they are the very different alternatives we face, opinion paper*. London: Sustainable Development Commission.

Dyer, J. H., Gregersen, H. B., & Christensen, C. M. (2009). The innovator's DNA. *Harvard Business Review, 87*, 60–67.

Fishback, B. (2009). A new model to catalyze a movement of high-growth entrepreneurs. In Kauffman Thought book 2009 (pp 52–56). Kansas City: Ewing Marion Kauffman Foundation

Goldstein, J., Hazy, J., & Lichtenstein, B. (2010). *Complexity and the nexus of leadership*. London: Palgrave Macmillan.

Isenberg, D. (2010). The big idea: How to start an entrepreneurial revolution. *Harvard Business Review, 88*, 40–50.

Johansson, F. (2006). *The medici effect: What elephants and epidemics can teach us about innovation*. Boston: Harvard Business School Press.

Pasieka, D. (2010). Do I need a coach, a mentor or both? Cedarvue Partners. Retrieved April 09 2010, from www.cedarvue.blogspot.com

Reeves, M., Sahla, H., & Bokkering, M. (2010). *Simulation advantage*. Boston: BCG Perspectives.

Skidelski, R. (2009). *Keynes. The return of the master*. New York: PublicAffairs.

Sloane, P. (2010). Create a culture of successful failure, contribution to 'Blogging Innovation'. http://www.businessstrategy-innovation.com/wordpress/2010/05/create-a-cultureof-successfull-failure/

Taleb, N. N. (2007). *The black swan*. New York: Random House.

Wuthrich, H. A. (1999). *'Achieving global competitiveness', in Handbook of Management*. London: Financial Times/Prentice Hall.

Chapter 7
Experiencing Experiments: A Multiplayer Game for Sharing Ideas: Crusoe Gives Way to Gulliver

Martin Curley and Piero Formica

For the things we have to learn before we can do them, we learn by doing them.

Aristotle

Introduction

Participants in laboratory experiments start a real business rather than just learning about business with cases or taking part in business games and role plays. The focus is on how to ensure that the reality does not fall short of what the experimenter desires. Any aspiring entrepreneur can experience experiments by adopting, in different combinations, "Robinson Crusoe" and "Lemuel Gulliver" behavioural modes, as described below.

These fictional characters from eighteenth century novels were chosen to characterize the types because of their very different experiences of learning

M. Curley · P. Formica (✉)
Technology and Business Innovation, National University of Ireland, Maynooth, Co. Kildare, Ireland
e-mail: piero.formica@gmail.com

M. Curley
Innovation Value Institute, National University of Ireland, Maynooth, Co. Kildare, Ireland
e-mail: martin.g.curley@intel.com

Intel Labs Europe, Collinstown Business Park, Leixlip, Co. Kildare, Ireland

P. Formica
Master in Entrepreneurship and Technology Management, University of Tartu, Tartu, Estonia

International Entrepreneurship Academy, Via Altaseta 3, 40123 Bologna, Italy

M. Curley and P. Formica (eds.), *The Experimental Nature of New Venture Creation*, Innovation, Technology, and Knowledge Management, DOI: 10.1007/978-3-319-00179-1_7, © Springer International Publishing Switzerland 2013

and survival. The shipwrecked hero of Daniel Defoe's Robinson Crusoe (1719) learns and invents means of survival largely through his own reflections and personal experience, but he remains isolated on his desert island. Lemuel Gulliver, in Jonathan Swift's Gulliver's Travels (1726), on the other hand, learns and develops through his constant interaction with different beings and cultures.

The 'Robison Crusoe' type is an aspiring entrepreneur whose habits (depending on his or her disposition, pattern of behaviour, motivations, and attitudes to entrepreneurship) exclude the influence of peers, for example through an absence of strategic interaction. In pure Crusoe mode, the experimenter gains experience practising experiments in an isolated environment. Crusoe has to make do without other people. This means that he or she is constrained by artificially boundaries, shows no interest in interaction and believes that costs exceed benefits of interactions such as talking to and learning from other experimenters. Using an analogy from Physics, 'Crusoe' exhibits the effects of the Heisenberg's Uncertainty Principle, being simultaneously unaware of both the value and momentum of a venture.

Unlike Crusoe, the 'Lemuel Gulliver' type is a would-be entrepreneur who confers a primary role on intensive and laborious interactions with peers from different cultural and business background. All participants focus on building their company—which fosters comradeship and shared understanding. In the Gulliver pure mode, the experimenter fully exploits the potential of interaction. The assumption is the more they are connected, the more intensive are dialogue and discussion, conflict, disagreement and the questioning of the existing premises, and the more they can gain experience by combining knowledge and insights from experiments conducted by networked peers.[1] The corollary to this assumption is that a Gulliver-type experimenter embedded in a wide and diverse range of their peer population has greater chances to ride the waves of changes and achieving creative breakthroughs from experiencing experiments. Thus, in effect, Heisenberg's Uncertainty Principle can be somewhat negated, because the close interaction with other researchers eliminates much of the uncertainty and there is then a far greater ability to simultaneously measure both the value and projected momentum of a nascent venture.

Experiment-Possibility Frontier

The experimental lab creates patterns that connect aspiring entrepreneurs with different ideas and personalities: it connects the 'Crusoes' and the 'Gullivers'. By experiencing experiments in a participative environment of open innovation for

---

[1] Gulliver types' decision-making process looks like the behavioural pattern of animal flocks such as birds and ants, "which often move in unison and make unanimous decisions at a moment's notice" (see *ScienceDaily*, September 16, 2010).

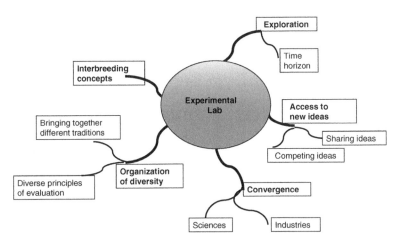

Fig. 1 Experimental lab: a participative environment of open innovation for entrepreneurship

entrepreneurship (Fig. 1), they learn whether and how the same idea could be used in different fields. To take advantage from the multiplier effect of sharing[2] —"I am going to use my idea in my field of use, and you are welcome to use it in your own field"—the Crusoes must give their up bad habits from working in a closed environment in favour of interaction. I doing so, they will have to bear the opportunity cost measured by the number of 'units' of the 'Crusoe's habits' forgone for one or more 'units' of the 'Gulliver's habit'.

[Open innovation is a paradigm that assumes that firms can and should use external ideas as well as internal ideas, and internal and external paths to market, as the firms look to advance their technology (Chesbrough 2003)]

Economies of experience, which in the experimental lab environment are the equivalent of the experience curve in manufacturing, reverse the upward trend in the cost curves (both the cost of experimentation and the opportunity cost of interaction). In fact, the more often experiencing experiments are performed, the lower is the cost of doing them; and the longer Crusoe personalities benefit from the opportunity to work in team with Gullivers, the more they unlock their potential, transform their specialised resources from Crusoe-use to Gulliver-use, and therefore achieve a decreasing opportunity cost of interaction. When experiments are run numerous times, even the Crusoes, individually very productive, give way to and turn into Gullivers (Fig. 2).

---

[2] According to the first law of knowledge dynamics, "knowledge multiplies when shared. The resulting knowledge energy is manifested through a broad range of mechanisms that includes Innovation Management, Leadership for Value Creation, Knowledge Pattern Recognition, Knowledge Mapping, Knowledge Networks, Social Cybernetics, Mental Models, Situation-Handling, and Capital Systems. Since knowledge is inherently a human process, we must take care to optimise its creation and flow in ways that minimize loss in the transmission process" (Amidon et al. 2006).

The stories of Crusoe and Gulliver can thus be used as metaphors for the very significant shift that is happening in innovation and entrepreneurship processes and environments. We are moving quickly from a closed innovation process through an open innovation process to a scenario where competing innovation networks become the norm. Sustained success results from contributing to and benefiting from a network or ecosystem which continuously creates new value and has higher velocity than other innovation networks: witness the growth of the Apple iPhone/App store and Google Android ecosystems. Aspiring entrepreneurs attaching to these ecosystems can benefit from the velocity of these ecosystems and experience the creativity that is continuously being unleashed.

At the core of Chesbrough's (2003) open innovation concept is the notion that innovation can be made more efficient and effective by the sharing of ideas and intellectual property between organisations in a controlled environment. Chesbrough, in his seminal book, focuses his open innovation thinking on established organisations. There is great value to be gained in extending this concept to early stage entrepreneurs.

Samelin et al. (2011) argue that a new form of open innovation is emerging which involves all actors in the ecosystem; others have recommended taking a broader view of networking, in order to take better advantage of societal capital at the disposal of firms. Extending this idea, networking and collaboration should be able to take optimal advantage of a particular ecosystem's capital.

Conducting experiments to determine potential outcomes and to ascertain the possible range of reactions of customers and other ecosystem stakeholders

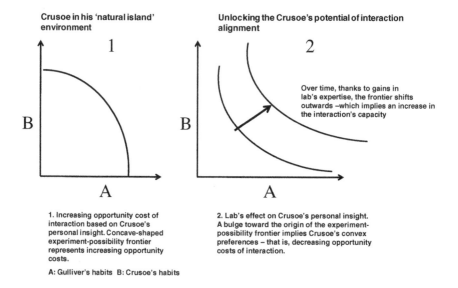

Fig. 2 The Crusoe-type experimenter's perception of the experiment-possibility frontier before an after engagement in an experimental lab network

to potential new ideas and innovations can be of significant value. Sharing these ideas between trusted collaborators can reduce uncertainty and provide guidance on the likelihood of success or indicate where changes of strategy may be needed. Indeed, the synaptic firing which can occur between entrepreneurs can lead to rapidly improving ideas. As well as using interpersonal and interorganisational conversations for experiments it is likely that Game Theory can accelerate the experimentation and learning process.

Game Theory embedded in software can model human and ecosystem organisation behaviour. It is often based on assumptions about how humans and organisations will react to changes or innovations based on what they perceive are in their best interest. This is a version of the invisible hand to which Adam Smith refers in his "Wealth of Nations". A key use of Game Theory might be to help assess where value would be captured in an ecosystem when a new innovation, or product or service, is introduced. A new venture or innovation may be only sustainable if a win–win scenario is created for other members in the ecosystem (but not necessarily competitors).

By assigning a value to the estimated utility of a potential innovation compared to the normalised value created by the existing materials, products and services in an ecosystem, and then estimating the probability of adoption, rebuttal or even counter initiatives by ecosystem stakeholders (including end-users), and running multiple simulation runs, some uncertainty can be removed from the entrepreneurial process. For estimating where value could be created, a portfolio optimisation schema such as that advocated by Von Neumann and Morgenstern (1944) could be used and then solved through linear programming to identify where the most value might arise across stakeholders. This finding could then be applied in formulating a strategy to leverage the ecosystem for the entrepreneurial activity.

The Value of Conversion: Venturing into Physics

Entrepreneurship goes beyond the manner (*nómos*) of dispensing a business idea. It has a real nature (*physis*) visible in the process of conversion (transmutation) of input into output resources, which occurs through 'entrepreneurial reaction'. When we look closely at how the process works for high-expectation and high-growth start-ups, which move at a lightning speed, there is a need to examine the 'reaction' on a very small scale. The principles and lessons that emerge from such an examination will be far more important than writing a formal and static document such as a business plan.

In this context, the entrepreneurial reaction examined through the lens of experiencing experiments leads to the exploration of an emerging science—'econophysics',[3] as it has been dubbed, which employs the tools from physics to study markets. Specifically,

---

[3] The term 'econophysics' has been coined by Harry Eugene Stanley in 1994 to denote the field of physics dealing with phenomena in economic fluctuations and finance. See Mantegna and Stanley (2000).

Fig. 3 The atomic structure
of an entrepreneurial creation

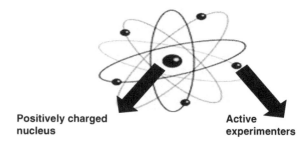

Positively charged   **Active**
nucleus   **experimenters**

the subfield devoted to the analysis of reaction highlights microscopic elements whose configuration resembles atomic structure.

Although at first sight the attempt to explain the entrepreneurial process in terms of the scientific discipline of physics may appear too contrived, there is be some insight to be gained in an analogy between business ideas, the units of entrepreneurship and atoms, the units of matter. At the centre (the 'nucleus') of a new venture creation, there is a positively charged idea whose initiator has to make sense of it and construct a vision. Almost all of its 'mass' is made up of strongly interactive, not easy distinguishable 'particles'—the motivations and attributes[4] in entrepreneurial behaviour (see Table 1 in Carayannis and Formica 2006)—in the 'nucleus' around which active experimenters are arranged in orbits. The orbiting experimenters are responsible for the 'chemical' properties of the idea, such as practicality, profitability, sustainability and so on (Fig. 3).

[*Note* This is the popularised image of an atom. It was created in 1904 by Hantaro Nagaoka (1865–1950), a Japanese pioneer of physics, who developed the planetary model of the atom (Bryson 2003)]

It is necessary for the 'particles' of motivations and attributes to be placed in an 'magnetic' entrepreneurial field and gain entrepreneurial energy, which is the capacity to do entrepreneurial work, in order to effect the transitions from the state of entrepreneurial intention to that of entrepreneurial action. 'Entrepreneurial energy' (E) and 'mass' (M) are two sides of the same coin. The cube of creativity (C) in business—that is, (creativity in technology) × (creativity in process) × (creativity in marketing)—is the conversion rate between the two. The Gulliver spirit of free discussions, open criticism and wide collaboration within the experimental lab enhances the speed of creativity, which is "like a beam of light that spotlights one or more opportunities to start a business" (Box 1).

---

[4] Entrepreneurial motivations encompass:
- Capacity to think for oneself,
- Self-confidence: optimism and personal drive,
- Sense of autonomy, independence and risk-taking,
- Intense emotions.
  Entrepreneurial attributes include:
- Clarity of leadership,
- Openness and inquisitiveness, stimulating innovation and learning,
- Ability to create new value or organsational capability.

Box 1: The 'Triadic Complex' of Entrepreneurial Attributes and Motivations and Creativity in Business

$E = MC^3$

where E is the entrepreneurial energy; M the attributes and motivations necessary for entrepreneurship and C^3 creativity in business.

Components of M:
Entrepreneurial attributes
Clarity of leadership
Openness and inquisitiveness, stimulating innovation and learning
Ability to create new value or organisational capability
Flexibility and capacity to change
Relationship-building skills
Ability to convince others (employees, individual investors, suppliers and landlords) to share start-up risks

Entrepreneurial motivations
Capacity to think for oneself
Self-confidence: optimism and personal drive
Sense of autonomy, independence and risk-taking
Intense emotions

Components of C^3:
Creativity in business = creativity in technology × creativity in planning × creativity in marketing
Note C is the equivalent of the speed of light. C in Latin is *Celeritas*, meaning 'velocity'. Creativity in business is like a beam of light that spotlights one or more opportunities to start up a business
Source Carayannis and Formica (2006)

An entrepreneurial reaction takes place when the 'nucleus' undergoes some kind of change, releasing the energy needed to transform business ideas into real ventures. In experimental labs, people from different industries and professions look at what one of them is doing with fresh eyes, and most changes occur through the adaptation and reinterpretation of one person's unfettered ideas in response to other people's ideas. By building upon one another's ideas, participants in experimental labs thus increase the number of ideas that can develop successfully. Strong networks of people freely exchanging ideas are made possible by decreasing the opportunity costs of interaction and an increasing the capacity for interaction (see the right-hand graph in Fig. 2). For a small input into a network, a large output of entrepreneurial outcomes can be produced.

When the nascent entrepreneur approaches an existing innovation ecosystem with a strong focus on experimentation, this can create the conditions for an experimental outcome which will catalyse an autocatalytic reaction, spurring subsequent and derivative innovation. Schumpter (1911) introduced the concept of innovation being associated as associated with a production function, with progress coming from a new intelligent combination of production means and production conditions. What better way to explore new intelligent combinations that exploit emerging technologies than to have active experimentation and continuous dialog? High expectation entrepreneurs should look for a host vertical industry, in which they can see opportunities for intersectional innovation. Here we see the "Medici effect" as described by Johansson (2006), in which significant and breakthrough innovations happen at the intersection of different industries and disciplines. Amazon provides examples of these disruptive game-changing innovations, first with its new bookselling business model and then with the Amazon Kindle for electronic book distribution. Both these innovations have dramatically accelerated the adoption and diffusion of information products (books). Amazon's continued progress through the development of its EC2 cloud platform demonstrates how experimentation leads to further progress.

Marc Andreessen, the co-inventor of Mosaic, claims that "Software is eating the world" (Economist, September, 2011). This is a description of the phenomenon we observe as Moore's Law collides with a virtual domain. Aspiring entrepreneurs would do well to examine the full value chain effects of this "digitization" process to identify areas of best opportunity.

While traditional factors such as access to finance, the regulatory environment, leadership and management skills and availability of a workforce and associated skills are important for successful entrepreneurship, soft vectors such as "social connectivity and networking" are, increasingly, becoming real differentiators for entry into an ecosystem; or indeed creation of a new ecosystem.

The Decoupling Hypothesis

In line with the stream of thought prevailing in the incubation industry, business idea and business plan are coupled together. The former is like an ocean liner that has to leave the harbour (i.e., the incubator). The latter is the tugboat pulling the ship out of the port. In the couple, business idea is the dependent element. In fact, to get to open water, it must rely on the perfunctory procedures and calculations of the business plan.

Serial entrepreneur Shai Agassi has drawn parallels between principles of business and the laws of physics to emphasise "the importance of acting on an idea before it's adopted by the mainstream and navigating the inevitable uncertainties that can result in success or failure".[5] Following this stream of thought, the hypothesis underlying the exercise of experiencing experiments is that each and every business idea is decoupled and independent from the business plan. High-expectation aspiring

[5] See http://ecorner.stanford.edu/author/shai_agassi

entrepreneurs are early birds in the marketplace. They experience the multilayered reality as well as the irreducible uncertainty of a market that does not yet exist or is still in its infancy. This state of affairs requires a multilayered endeavour as well as consideration of probability, rather than the usual coupled method based on 'I do my best to ensure my idea is the one that wins out' and 'I stay with the certain measurement of my business plan'.

On the one hand, with Crusoe who gives way to Gulliver, a lower intellectual resistance to shifting direction reinforces the motivation to build one idea on another until a breakthrough is reached and "before it's adopted by the mainstream". In the experimental labs, two or more nuclei of business ideas come into very close contact with each other, and it is possible that they fuse together to produce unusual findings that fall outside the existing categories.

On the other hand, it is looking at the distribution of business ideas through the glass of quantum physics that it is possible to identify the marketplace destination of a business idea. Laying down the *probability*, the *probably*, or the *likely* distribution of 'quantum packets' of business ideas with different amounts of entrepreneurial energy uncovers the answer to 'how to innovate effectively'. This is a major task the experimental lab has to accomplish.

Whilst the Crusoe type person is justifiably concerned with the predation (i.e., the stealing of ideas) that might take place in an experimental lab, it would appear that the benefits of co-opetition and symbiosis should outweigh the downsides of possible predation. In the experimental lab one should experience a high level of interaction resonance, enhanced through a richness of information flow. The experimental lab is a vital living lab where the exchanges of energy, ideas and indeed part-resources are numerous, vital and sustainable. Many believe that relationships are the foundation of all accomplishments and the experimental lab is based on this principle. Also Sveiby (1997) has said that trust is the bandwidth of communication and in a well-managed experimental lab with enough diversity of raw ventures, high trust and strong relationships may well manifest themselves. In the experimental lab, the new innovations and ventures are outcomes of the innovation ecosystem where the interaction of processes, resources, ideas create a living ecology. This living ecology can be a virtualised one with distributed physical resources and locations contributing.

The Theory in Practice: A Case Example

The discourse on experiencing experiments has brought us close to interlocutors eager to scale up their entrepreneurial expectations. They are pre-eminently aspiring entrepreneurs whose high impulse to innovate qualify them as "economic activists". Herewith we give evidences of how one of these interlocutors has lived the experience of setting up his own business from the standpoint of an active experimenter.

Nicola Farronato graduated in business at Cà Foscari University in Venice and founder of the open network Young European Avant-garde Minds, was in his 10th year of work anniversary when he was wondering how to make a greater impact in what he was doing. In his own words, "Up to that moment, many times I have been told I had a greater potential. Each and every of those times my expectations were scaling up, but looking around where I was and which kind of shift I could do, I found myself not able to effectively unleash my innovation energy".

Something changed the day Nicola found inspiration in the role played by the knowledge-driven entrepreneurs (Andersson et al. 2010) whom he was eager to identify with. This was the key to opening him the door of both Intentac (International Entrepreneurship Academy—www.intentac.org) and IVI (Innovation Value Institute—www.ivi.ie) ecosystems. "It was the beginning of 2009 when—says Nicola—I started to get closer to the partners and members of this interactive ecology, in which at the beginning I was relying mainly for networking purposes. In few months the Intentac and IVI ecosystems have accelerated the extension of my entrepreneurship and innovation network, as well as my shift from business developer to would-be entrepreneur".

Nicola has made it a habit to profit from the experiencing experiments formula, combined with the access to a number of high level fellows of both Intentac and IVI networks. "Being at my first experience as entrepreneur—Nicola has asserted—I had a lot to learn and could not wait too long to step into the journey, even if everything appeared uncertain. The overall economic contingency and the heavy drop of demand across 2009 and 2010 seemed to be not promising for starting a new business. Notwithstanding this, lean start-up and learning-by-doing through experimentation looked like the best approaches to spurring entrepreneurial energy".

Leaving in Italy and travelling often to Ireland to follow the epicentre of the experimentation activities surrounding both Intentac and IVI at the National University of Ireland, Nicola has brought in place a tough decision on the entrepreneurship platform to adopt. Having a digital idea to turn into a web start-up, he wanted to blend brand & design culture with a highly tech environment. Finally, Nicola resolved to start his own business in Dublin, an entrepreneurial environment close to his vision, supportive to a lean start-up and central to the experimentation practices.

"Our business process development—Nicola argues—was well in place, trying to get continuous feedback from the stakeholders we were daily connecting with. We have got a lot of support in our early days in Dublin with the backing of peers and other active experimenters in the Intentac-IVI ecology, and we have been able to gain a pre-seed funding and mentoring through the LaunchPad program at NDRC (National Digital Research Center—see Box 2). We have been the first international team admitted to this early-stage acceleration program and we are considered among the first overseas entrepreneurs starting-up in Ireland after the financial crisis".

Box 2: National Digital Research Centre: From Ideas to Income

"The National Digital Research Centre (NDRC) is an Irish independent enterprise dedicated to practical, market value focused innovation.

Start-up experiments are made at the NDRC's Inventorium, which is a "programme designed to find innovative digital ideas and turn them into sustainable businesses. [By] providing spaces for engagement and collaboration across sectors, communities and disciplines, and focusing on open innovation, Inventorium works with participants at events, but also with people who contact them directly. NDRC's Inventorium helps bring together the teams and mix of skills needed to accelerate great ideas".

Source NDRC Annual Report 2010–2011

B-sm@rk Ltd, Dublin—the company co-founded in 2010 by Nicola—is a start-up with expectation for exponential growth, which aims to launch a revolutionary marketing service (Box 3). Nicola's experience journey that led to B-sm@rk first product, MySmark, is represented in Fig. 4.

The formula for experiencing experiments is driving the company's founder to steer and validate his business idea in the shortest time possible, using efficiently personal resources and any other funding scheme available. Through the experience gained by participating in experiments, Nicola has learnt how to conduct a multiplayer game for the purpose of building upon one another's ideas. He has

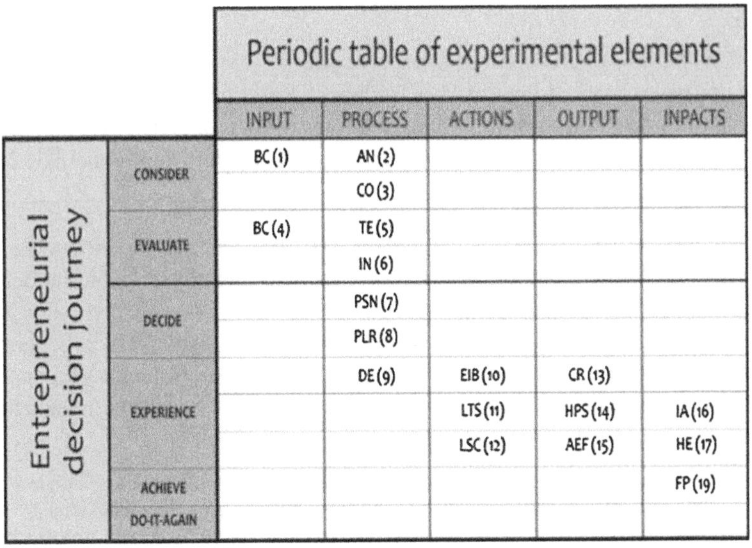

Periodic table of experimental elements					
		INPUT	PROCESS	ACTIONS	OUTPUT	INPACTS

Entrepreneurial decision journey		INPUT	PROCESS	ACTIONS	OUTPUT	INPACTS
	CONSIDER	BC (1)	AN (2)			
			CO (3)			
	EVALUATE	BC (4)	TE (5)			
			IN (6)			
	DECIDE		PSN (7)			
			PLR (8)			
	EXPERIENCE		DE (9)	EIB (10)	CR (13)	
				LTS (11)	HPS (14)	IA (16)
				LSC (12)	AEF (15)	HE (17)
	ACHIEVE					FP (19)
	DO-IT-AGAIN					

Fig. 4 MySmark business process development versus Nicola's experience journey. See the key in Fig. xxx in Chap. 4

also learnt how to build an entrepreneurial option, different from the original one, through a fluid deployment of flexile and interactive teams.

In order to pursue sustainability and maintaining a smart approach towards innovation, Nicola is setting up collaboration agreements with a number of tech universities in Europe, thus involving post-graduate students with the company's operations in Ireland. As Nicola puts it, "Diaspora entrepreneurship is part of the international brain circulation that enhances our business idea by attracting partners from all over the world. Diversity is a critical asset in our organization. It brings added value when talking about cross-fertilization between cultures and domains".

Box 3: The Theory in Practice: B-Smark's *Smart Mark*

"A year to the day after being formed, digital media company B-Smark has launched a public beta of its first product, an online service that lets people attach an emotional tag to content on social networks. The company has also beefed up its advisory board with experienced marketers and entrepreneurs.

MySmark is the company's first product, a digital *smart mark* people can use on friends, links, posts, photos, events and videos that have been posted on social networks. The service is initially available for Facebook and Twitter, with other social platforms planned.

The 'Like' button for interacting with content is anonymous—MySmark is a layer above that," says B-Smark co-founder Nicola Farronato.

Users create their profile at MySmark.com, with an individual smart mark in the form of a flower-shaped widget consisting of 32 emotions. They can then register any of those moods about a piece of content and share it online.

Farronato says the attraction for a brand, product or service is that they can use smart marks to get market feedback in real time".

Source Gordon Smith, "B-Smark allows users to attach emotional tag to content", *The Irish Times*, Friday, September 23, 2011

Albeit it is still a matter for judgement, Nicola's experience shows the evolutionary nature of experimental labs. Confronted with the conventional model of the incubator, laboratory experiments are a subject of great controversy today. Yet, we suggest that the process of experiencing in a multiplayer game, which generates the content of experience, is both desirable and possible. Experimental lab capabilities making practicable that process would be of a great benefit to the raising up of a new breed of high-expectation entrepreneurs.

(1) BC: Nicola's entrepreneurial journey entrepreneurial journey started with a rough initial idea of subjective satisfaction which aimed at providing individuals a tool to instantly identify the level of personal satisfaction with regards to people, things and places. This idea has been the core input of the business process development of MySmark in the form of a **business concept**.

(2) AN: the process of considering to start-up begun with an **analogical** approach towards the creation of a new company. Looking at what and how other entrepreneurs

were creating start-up companies has been very important to understand analogies in terms of opportunities and threats of the project.

(3) CO: aiming to do real innovation meant well considering what others were doing but was not enough though. A lot of uncertainty was raising around unexplored areas of the business idea. It has been very important to adopt also a **conjectural** approach to build the new project framework step by step, using an experimental behaviour.

(4) BC: the entrepreneurial journey of Farronato started maturing after some revisions of the initial business concept. A more structured entrepreneurial evaluation phase needed to pull together all the relevant information and assumptions gathered until that moment and turn on an enhanced **business concept**.

(5) TE: also the business idea turned mature for an initial test to be conducted with friends and a limited test users base. Even if the first attempts were quite sterile, **testing** was really helpful to make small choices in an uncertain decision process.

(6) IN: alpha tests of the business idea were built on a mobile basic interaction: a user could register emotional responses and value satisfaction by a codified SMS vocabulary. Tests led to a lot of **investigation** on user's interaction and understanding of the tool.

(7) PSN: even if the business concept was still a very high-level thought, Farronato was really committed to make it happen. **Participating to social networks** of entrepreneurs and innovators on an international scale was in that moment accelerating his mindset towards his entrepreneurial decision.

(8) PLR: the more the business process development was maturing the more Nicola was placed under realistic conditions of the start-up project in its business concept experimentation.

(9) DE: all the experiments, feedback, insights shared and interactions matured the **decision** to create a new company with high expectations of growth. The decision to become formally an entrepreneur was a breakthrough for Farronato in that moment. The company was incorporated in Ireland, right at the centre of Intentac experimental labs.

(10) EIB: the nature of the entrepreneurial behaviour of Farronato was **experiment induced**. After some failed attempts of creating a new company to make innovation, MySmark project was finally conducive for him to enter the innovative entrepreneurs ecosystem.

(11) LTS: MySmark project has been bootstrapped at the beginning by Farronato and his business partners. The lean start-up approach pushed them to **accelerate the start-up launch** as much as possible. After 1 month from the incorporation, MySmark has been chosen by a top pre-seed investor in Ireland to be accelerated.

(12) LSC: 12 weeks had to be sufficient to achieve a minimum viable product (MVP), start piloting it and get market feedback. To **keep the start-up cost low** MySmark MVP has been developed by talented junior computer scientists, thanks to a collaboration agreement pushed by Farronato with an italian university.

(13) CR: the lean start-up approach along with early stage strategic collaborations **lowered the need for upfront capital** by MySmark. The first move of the new company has been smoothly governed, and the shareholders structure could develop harmonised.

(14) HPS: MySmark has been the winner of an investment prize based on its MVP after the 3 months take-off. The achievement has been mainly due to a good fit in between the innovation proposition and the MVP execution and pivoting. This prize has opened **new opportunities for the start-up to get underway** and go-to-market.

(15) AEF: the experimental approach adopted by Farronato and his team in the MySmark project could show some **advantages in terms of results**, especially if compared with different approaches based on predictions and complex business planbusiness planning. Once again a lean approach combined with an experimental process have helped MySmark in its development process and go-to-market.

(16) IA: MySmark team has soon started to **seek industrial partners** in order to accelerate go-to-market and leverage its lean architecture. Being positioned as an innovative marketing platform, MySmark has attracted interest from market research players, Web service providers and international brands willing to join its business programme.

(17) HE: thanks to the investments and early adopters commercial activity, MySmark could **hire employees** after 6 months of operations, and grow them to 5 full time after 12 months of operations.

(18) SF: **support from financiers** is a great opportunity when really needed. MySmark approach has been focused on maturing the business concept as much as possible before raising a real serious round of investment. There has been no support from financiers to get to first paying customer and product trials.

(19) FP: MySmark is currently in the phase of fund raising its first investment round in order to support a wide scale business concept validation with international brands. Farronato and his team are currently evaluating **funding opportunities** in Europe and US as well as **industrial strategic collaborations**.

References

Amidon, D., Formica, P., & Mercier-Laurent, E. (Eds.). (2006). *Knowledge economics: Emerging principles, practices and policies* (Vol. 1), Introduction. Tartu: Tartu University Press.

Andersson, T., Curley, G. M., & Formica, P. (2010). *Knowledge-driven entrepreneurship: The key to social and economic transformation.* New York: Springer.

Bryson, B. (2003). A short history of nearly everything. Broadways Books.

Carayannis, E. G., & Formica, P. (2006, June). Intellectual venture capitalists: An emerging breed of knowledge entrepreneurs. *Industry & Higher Education, 20*(3), 151–156.

Chesbrough, H. W. (2003). *Open innovation: The new imperative for creating and profiting from technology* (p. xxiv). Boston: Harvard Business School Press.

Johansson, F. (2006). The medici effect: breakthrough insights at the intersection of ideas, concepts, and cultures. MA, Boston: Harvard Business School Press.

Mantegna, R. N., & Stanley, H. E. (2000). *An introduction to econophysics: Correlation and complexity in finance.* Cambridge: Cambridge University Press.

Samelin, B., Curley, M., Honka, A., Sadowska, A., & OISPG (2011). *Service innovation yearbook.* EU Publications.

Schumpter, J. (1911). Theorie der wirtschaftlichen entwicklung (transl. 1934, the theory of economic development: An inquiry into profits, capital, credit, interest and the business cycle. Transaction Publishers).

Sveiby, K. E. (1997). *The new organizational wealth: Managing and measuring knowledge-based assets.* San Francisco: Berrett-Koehler.

Von Neumann, J., & Morgenstern, O. (1944). *Theory of games and economic behaviour.* Princeton: Princeton University Press.

Part II
Enhancing Experiments in New Venture Creation: The Entrepreneurial Student Perspective

Chapter 8
What's New in the Launching of Start-Ups? Features and Implications of Laboratory Experiments

Diego Matricano

The man with a new idea is a crank—until the idea succeeds.
Mark Twain, American author, 1835–1910.

Introduction

The profound changes that have occurred in the economic environment over the last few years have led to increasingly intense competition among business enterprises. Identifying how best new companies can be launched and sustained in this new competitive environment is a key challenge for entrepreneurs and educators alike.

The experimental laboratory approach to new ventures as a means of launching high-expectation start-ups combines old and new concepts. It is derived from the incubator model but, unlike that model, is not concerned with the offering of 'physical' services, such as offices and communication facilities, but rather with 'virtual' services, such as knowledge and experience. It takes common industry practices, which have been in use for many years—like rapid prototyping and testing, concurrent management (based on repeated iterations, updates and revisions) and co-development with customers and partners, and adapts them to and locates them in the pre-launch experimental lab. The aim is to make a connection between the development of new business ideas (of primary importance) with the practical reality of the business environment.

In this chapter, we investigate the three steps of laboratory development (experiment, simulation, clinical treatment) and the exposure mode applied to the idea (that

D. Matricano (✉)
Istituto di Ricerche sulle Attività Terziare (IRAT), Naples, Italy
e-mail: diego.matricano@gmail.com

via A. De Gasperi, n. 83, 81055 Santa Maria Capua Vetere, CE, Italy

M. Curley and P. Formica (eds.), *The Experimental Nature of New Venture Creation*,
Innovation, Technology, and Knowledge Management, DOI: 10.1007/978-3-319-00179-1_8,
© Springer International Publishing Switzerland 2013

of conjecture, or trial, as opposed to analogy, or case study) through experiments in collaboration, some interesting issues emerge. We consider the appropriateness of the model to the new economic environment and look, in particular, at the role of experts in assessing new business ideas and the transition to the notion of entrepreneurship as something that can be nurtured as opposed to something that is innate.

The New Economic Context

The new economic setting is characterized by globalization, a continuous influx of technological innovation and intense competition. These factors not only make the competition between existing companies more and more difficult but, above all, make the launching of a new venture increasingly risky and complex. The average failure rate of start-ups is over 50 %, but it rises to 80 % for high-tech start-ups. The implication of such statistics is that the old process of new venture creation, based on the paradigm of 'technology–business–funding' (see Box 1) is no longer appropriate.

That 'technology–business–funding' model concentrated on the creation of a business related to a newly discovered technology. The economic setting was comparatively static, a long way from the rapidly increasing competitiveness of today's environment, and markets grew constantly, fueled by productivity. It required very high ability to secure funds to launch and develop a new business. And the extent of the funds available would often make the difference between a successful and unsuccessful business. This model still persists in some industries: the biotechnology, nanotechnology, and green-technology sectors are still capital-intensive and the cost of starting a business is very high. But for many sectors the old model no longer reflects the reality, and for Internet-based start-ups it is simply anachronistic.

A new paradigm, therefore, more appropriate for the new economic context, must be developed. Technology (that is, the idea) is still the most important driver of the world economy, even if how we approach it has changed. In the past, new technological discoveries were comparatively few and far between. Now, however, technologies are commodities. Incremental improvements are made to existing technologies frequently and very easily. So, although we acknowledge that technology is still the driving force we must locate it in a new paradigm.

A step-by-step identification of the differences between then and now is illuminating. First, the economic setting has changed radically. Funds have lost their primary importance: even if they remain important in developing a business, the brain now plays the main role. There are many recent examples of how the idea is more important than the funding (Amazon and Google are two obvious cases). This brings us to the new paradigm. After the discovery phase (the technology or idea), it is not useful to try to develop a business model: this comes later. In a context of continuous change, a new business cannot be developed without a thorough consideration of the current and potential needs of others. The second phase of the paradigm may, rather, be the testing of the business idea to validate or reject it.

Examining the needs of others is not simple. We do not refer here only to the needs of recipients (market needs). Testing the business idea involves more than investigating what consumers want (what they are waiting and looking for): it includes many other considerations—looking at potential suppliers for input materials, organizing the production model, testing feasibility, estimating the likely chances of success, defining the opportunity cost of every choice made, evaluating possible alternatives, and then analyzing customers' needs. Testing the application of a discovered technology should be designed to identify the simplest solution (as in the KISS principle—'keep it simple, stupid') and this is the high-expectation entrepreneur's most difficult task. Only if the business idea can be developed in the simplest way, taking into account all the factors listed above, the entrepreneur can reach the final phase, which is the development of marketing plans and target sales.

In sum, the new paradigm should flow like this: 'technology/idea–idea testing–simplest solution–marketing/sales'. These four phases summarize the process through which a new idea can evolve into a new high-expectation start-up.

Box 1: The Case of Apple

In the late 1970s Steve Jobs, with Apple co-founder Steve Wozniak, created one of the first commercially successful personal computers. In the early 1980s, Jobs were among the first to see the commercial potential of the mouse-driven Graphical User Interface. In 1978, Mike Markkula of Apple Computers introduced Steve Jobs and Steve Wozniak to Arthur Rock and the subsequent Apple story is familiar to all.

This historical nugget is a good example of a strategy based on the paradigm 'technology–business–funding'. During the 1980s, on the one hand, the technology developed by Apple was characterized by ease of use, ease of configuration and integrated multimedia. On the other hand, people knew nothing about computers. The strategy worked successfully because the new technology was perfectly suited to the growing market demand for computers for private use and the funds needed to launch and develop the company were available.

A Metaphor

A comparison of hens and pigs helps to clarify the difference between the old and new business models. In the past, when the market was less competitive, the relatively few companies, the hens, had plenty of time to reflect on their new ideas, or eggs, and at the end of that brooding period the ideas might or might not be hatched. Some ideas, in the form of new products, services, or processes, were good enough to go to market without modification. Others had to be modified according to customers' needs, and this was feasible since the time to market was longer than it is now. Yet others had to be replaced. In the new economic setting, the scenario has changed radically. Many companies, operating in a crowded market, must develop successful ideas straight away because they will not have another chance. In this environment, the small new ventures are the pigs. After they have brought out a new product, service or process, they have two opportunities: they can be successful (live and grow fat) or failure (die). There is no other choice. This new market competition is based on the 'aut-aut' principle (drive the market or leave it), since investors have short expectations regarding returns on their investments and are always ready to cut their losses.

Who is Involved in Business Laboratory Experiments?

In light of the above discussion, we need to test whether the 'technology/idea–idea testing–simplest solution–marketing/sales' paradigm really works in this challenging new economic environment. The progression from analysis of needs to the search for the simplest solution is an iterative process. This is because the relationship between these two exercises is not linear. Evaluating the prototype, testing it, obtaining feedback and revising it are repeated continuously to refine the idea and find the best solution, and this iterative process requires specific skills that a would-be entrepreneur may not be able to develop himself or herself. This is why the experimental laboratory can play a decisive role in this essential stage of exploration, analysis, and definition. Since a laboratory involves skilled partners from different backgrounds, the business proposition can be examined from a variety of critical perspectives and its assumptions and predictions accordingly modified, revised, and refined until it is ready for market. These skilled partners may include people from universities, research centers, governments, non-governmental organizations, venture capital firms, fund-raising organizations, and the supply chain as well as customers and experienced entrepreneurs.

The main essence of activity in the experimental laboratory is diversity. Diversity is often critically lacking in new business idea development—an entrepreneur, for example, may 'fall in love' with his or her business idea and this makes a properly objective evaluation less likely. Different points of view, specific competences, different group thinking, and problem-solving teams with members from different backgrounds are the strength of experimental laboratories. This diversity constitutes a best practice approach to the preparation for market of high-expectation start-ups.

The relationship between the high-expectation entrepreneur and the laboratory partners is a critical factor in the establishment of a successful business lab. Potential weak points must be addressed to ensure that the best results emerge from the lab. The different backgrounds of the experts involved, a key asset in one respect, can be a significant problem in another respect. It is therefore important to clarify precisely how the laboratory will operate.

The groups involved in experimental laboratories are not created to make decisions by committee or to indulge in 'group-thinking'. Making a decision according to combined expert advice can be a recipe for mediocrity: thus ensuring that groups can work productively together is the main challenge. There are two distinct approaches toward forming a coherent unit from a group of disparate people. First, they can be made to feel they are fighting a common enemy. The other approach is to ensure that everyone knows that they are facing the same problem or, more broadly, that they have a common goal. In the case discussed here of assessing start-up potential, people can be effectively linked together via the second approach—the identification of a common goal requiring different inputs. The goal is to launch a successful start-up. The different motivations cohere toward that end. The would-be entrepreneur wants to be a successful entrepreneur, universities and research centers want to collaborate in technological progress and disseminate their knowledge and results, governments and non-governmental organizations want to improve people's quality of life, venture capitalists and fund-raisers want to create new businesses, suppliers want to develop new outlets, customers want to satisfy their needs. All these various motivations thus bind the participants together effectively in pursuit of the common goal of launching a new venture.

From Nature to Nurture

The experimental laboratory approach stresses the transition from the old approach, based on 'nature', to the new one, which is characterized by 'nurture'. This transition marks a shift in entrepreneurial strategy from pull to push.

The essence of nature versus nurture debate in relation to entrepreneurship is the perceived opposition between innate qualities and personal experience. The innate qualities are seen as causal factors in the would-be entrepreneur's desire to develop something in his or her own right. In this view, personal talents and persistence drive the entrepreneur to be successful. Thus the 'nature' argument works on the assumption that the entrepreneur is autonomous, aware of his or her knowledge, risk-taking, trial-oriented, able to change the setting in which she or he operates, forward-looking, confident of his or her own ability to overcome difficulties. This is a description of the neo-classical natural-born entrepreneur who, in fact, is a rare phenomenon. Most entrepreneurs need training.

The new economic setting is not a place for just a few idiosyncratic entrepreneurs. It is an environment that can 'create' more and more entrepreneurs. To enable this to happen, attention must focus on nurturing entrepreneurship, which involves providing the personal experiences through which would-be entrepreneurs can be encouraged, inspired, and helped to become effective actual entrepreneurs. Modern entrepreneurs recognize the advantages of personal networks: they are aware that they do not have all the knowledge they need and they try to reduce risks. They have a more prudent approach to facing problems because they know that rapid change can cause difficulties as well as opportunities. They monitor economic conditions carefully and lay stress on the careful management of relationships with colleagues and others in their networks. In summary, the new high-expectation entrepreneur has a new relationship to the market: it is the personal network that drives the evaluation of the new idea and by means of which it is evaluated.

As already noted, the shift from nature to nurture in entrepreneurship reflects a parallel strategic shift from pull to push. In the strategic approach characterized by 'pull', a would-be entrepreneur simply looks at what is missing in a market and tries to exploit the opportunity offered by the gap because he or she has an entrepreneurial instinct. In the strategic approach characterized by 'push', on the other hand, the entrepreneur is not looking for an existing gap. He or she is able to develop a new business idea that will modify the market for which it is destined: there is a strong conscious desire to be an entrepreneur.

The dichotomies between 'nature' and 'nurture' and 'pull' and 'push' lend weight to the notion of experimental laboratories as a means of launching high-expectation start-ups in the contemporary business environment. The transition in approach from nature to nurture reflects the adaptability and flexibility that an entrepreneur must now develop. The ultimate goal remains the same, but the process through which it is achieved is very different.

Future Implications

The essentially straightforward concept of experimental laboratories, then, may well be the best solution to the problems engendered by the new economic setting. The experimental laboratory approach draws a parallel between their idea and the traditional medical laboratory. This parallel, however, may be somewhat misleading, as the practices of the medical laboratory reflect only part of the business analysis process that the model of experimental laboratories for high-expectation entrepreneurs is designed to achieve. The medical laboratory does indeed serve as a useful illustration of the process that occurs when skilled participants in a business laboratory are involved in defining the simplest solution for a would-be entrepreneur, but it is not so relevant when it comes to the implementation of high-expectation start-ups. Translating the decisions of the laboratory experts into practical choices is the second part of the process.

Another, perhaps more complete, metaphor for the experimental laboratory approach is offered by Formula One. To win the whole competition, you need the best team:

- the best car designers (experts);
- the fastest car (the best products, processes, and services);
- a good starting point in the race (a good reputation).

At the same time you must put in place the best process, based on:

- changing the wheels to those best adapted to the surface (finding the best fit of the product to the market—facing the competition);
- using the pit stop when necessary (getting help at the right time);
- maximizing driving ability (maximizing entrepreneurial skills to keep in front of the competition).

The first three requirements are very close to the diagnostic goals of experimental laboratories. The last three activities, if put in place after a start-up has been launched, may well not be effective in curing the problem—and so they should be included among the key activities of the experimental phase.

Some issues do need to be addressed as the experimental lab model is developed. How, for example, is the period of 'virtual incubation' to be determined? If an experimental laboratory could continue to work on a start-up after its launch, the potential benefit to the entrepreneur could be even greater. Were this to happen, the virtual activity of the experimental laboratory could become the strongest and most sustaining link between entrepreneurial intention and entrepreneurial action.

Chapter 9
Resourcing Lab Experiments for New Ventures: The Potential of a Start-up Database

Alberto Pietrobon

> *Errors using inadequate data are much less than those using no data at all.*
> Charles Babbage, English Mathematician and Inventor, 1791–1871.

Introduction

In the past few decades, venture capitalists and business angels have typically financed start-ups based on new ideas and products. The proposal for a system of laboratory experiments is designed to provide new entrepreneurs not only with money, but also with experience and knowledge before they venture into the market. The main objectives are to minimize mistakes, to increase efficiency, and enable the entrepreneur to operate effectively from the very beginning. From this perspective, laboratory experiments should make it possible to reach positive results that otherwise could have been achieved only after several years of experience in the 'real world'.

Laboratory Experiments

We can define high-expectation start-ups as new companies that aim to introduce innovative and revolutionary new products or services into the marketplace. Such products and services will be technologically advanced and are likely to lead to the growth of high-tech industries. Entrepreneurs with these high expectations are

A. Pietrobon (✉)
Via Piave 23, Castelfranco Veneto, Veneto 31033, Italy
e-mail: alberto.pietrobon@se.ibm.com; albertopt@gmail.com

IBM Svenska AB, Stockholm, Sweden

M. Curley and P. Formica (eds.), *The Experimental Nature of New Venture Creation*, 93
Innovation, Technology, and Knowledge Management, DOI: 10.1007/978-3-319-00179-1_9,
© Springer International Publishing Switzerland 2013

willing to explore new areas of technology with fresh eyes, ideas, ambition, and energy. Unlike existing businesses, in which strategies and methods are already in place and are grounded in experience, high-expectation entrepreneurs develop innovative ideas and markets from scratch.

The basic idea of the proposed experimental laboratories is to simulate the real-life environment prior to the introduction of the product to the market. Here, 'simulation' involves evaluating the current state of the market, the industry, and the political system in order to predict the likely outcomes of decisions and the feasibility of various strategic actions. This process of evaluation is achieved through consultation with experts from a variety of backgrounds and through interaction with established companies, so that previous mistakes can be avoided. This sharing of experience will help to guide new entrepreneurs to make good decisions with respect to marketing campaigns, approaching potential new investors, interacting with policy makers, and many other aspects of doing business.

The aim behind the laboratory model, then, is to provide the new entrepreneur with the kind of experience and knowledge that are typically gained through years of experience of operating in real markets. The great advantage is that the experiments and simulations are done in a risk-free environment, in which where mistakes are positive lessons to be learned rather than the negative money-losing bad decisions they would be in the real market.

The experimental entrepreneurship process recalls the development process of clinical treatments in medicine: this traditional model is adapted and applied to experimentation with and treatment of business-related problems, in collaboration with private sector and public sector organizations. The process is a continuous iteration of 'examination–treatment–testing' steps until a working solution is established.

The process of gaining experience and knowledge in laboratories relates to a basic function of education. Many students attend university to gain knowledge about the field they have chosen for their future work, and they undertake internships to gain practical experience in that field. Why should the same approach not be applied to launching a new company? This is precisely what is proposed with the laboratory experiment model, which offers would-be entrepreneurs the opportunity to gain both knowledge and practical experience of their chosen business sector.

If the real-world market is envisaged as a crowded city, the entrepreneur is like a person who must navigate and explore that city for the first time. In the case of conventional venture capitalism, the entrepreneur easily becomes lost in the city, with pockets full of money but little idea where to go. The laboratory experiments provide maps and reveal shortcuts, giving the entrepreneur a sense of direction and the means to reach his or her goal in the quickest and best way.

IT in Support of Laboratory Experiments

When we read histories of successful companies, we gain many insights and much useful guidance—from such factors as how they hired and then motivated their employees or how they planned and implemented marketing campaigns, we acquire an understanding of the strategies and practices that led to the company's success. However, histories and biographies rarely take any, but the most successful companies and business people as their subjects. What if we could get access to the histories of all start-ups, even the smallest ones? And what if this information could be accessed with a few clicks of the mouse? This could constitute an invaluable for an entrepreneur considering a new business launch and in need of experience and advice.

Start-Up Database

A possible solution could be the creation of a database from which it would be possible to obtain precise details rapidly on a given certain group of companies— a database containing information on start-ups, both successful and unsuccessful, in which every company is categorized in various ways. For instance, a company could be categorized by business field, by country, by employee numbers, and by market. Information could be retrieved from the database with the help of search software and by refining category by category. Furthermore, such a database could also be a source of raw secondary data that could be used for additional research and statistics gathering.

The database could also provide a facility to compare a company's history with market trends. The visual timeline of Google Finance is an example. By creating a similar function, users would be able to select the companies they wished to analyse and then distinguish patterns and find indications that might lead to precious knowledge.

The main idea regarding this proposed database is not to provide a means of identifying two similar companies so they can be studied comparatively: this would not be feasible anyway, as high-expectation start-ups are innovative and unique. Rather, the central rationale for the database would be to be a source of information that will often be difficult to find for two reasons: location and accessibility. Besides, there are valuable lessons to be learned, and inspiration to be gained, from the histories of previous start-ups even if they are not closely related to the chosen business field of the potential entrepreneur. When researchers work on a project, for example, they are not inclined to search for a text that simply matches their own thoughts and ideas. They will locate and collect information from different sources and then, based on their analysis of that information, will complete the project by applying their own preferences and ideas. Hence, the aim of the database is to provide instant access to valuable information that is currently difficult to locate and access.

Possible Problems and Solutions

The data collection process would need to combine qualitative and quantitative techniques. The data would be acquired through questionnaire surveys and structured and in-depth interviews to elicit implicit and tacit knowledge. One key challenge is how to collect such a large amount of data for a large territory. This can best be achieved by continuously iterating the data collection process, with techniques and questionnaires continuously refined and ultimately optimized for the task. Problems of physical distance and other geographical obstacles can be overcome by data collection over the Internet, with no need for face-to-face interviews.

Another key concern relates to the availability of information, given that many companies will not be keen to share their history and strategies with potential new competitors. However, even though many at first might refuse the request, once it is becomes clear that what are sought are not hidden secrets and plans but simple facts about their history, the prospects of acquiring the information will surely increase.

Conclusions

Laboratories for high-expectation entrepreneurs could be enhanced by the creation of a start-up database. With the aid of instant access to historical facts of previously established businesses, the laboratory process they describe could be boosted and facilitated by yet another reliable source of information—of which the primary contributors would be the professionals involved. The creation of such a database clearly carries with it substantial challenges, both in terms of data collection and the appropriate format and structure of the data to ensure effective consultation. However, in the view of this author, the potential benefits to be gained from the substantial sharing of experience it would provide more than justify further exploration and investigation of the idea.

Chapter 10
Experimental Labs for Start-ups: The Role of the 'Venture-Sitter'

Diego Matricano and Alberto Pietrobon

> *Innovation opportunities do not come with the tempest but with the rustling of the breeze.*
>
> Peter Drucker, social ecologist, 1909–2005.

Introduction

This Chapter examines the advantages that high-expectation entrepreneurs can derive from participating in 'experimental laboratories' for business with regard to specifically practical implementation. Although experimental business labs can indeed enhance performance, promote the development of entrepreneurial skills, and reduce operating costs, questions remain as to how best to initiate the process and what means can be used to make it work effectively.

The knowledge Market

Markets are characterized by the forces of and balance between demand and supply. This applies to the knowledge market as it does to all others, but the continuous development of new knowledge makes this market unique in other ways.

D. Matricano (✉)
Istituto di Ricerche sulle Attività Terziare—I.R.A.T, via A. De Gasperi, n. 83, 81055 Santa Maria Capua Vetere (CE), Italy
e-mail: diego.matricano@gmail.com

A. Pietrobon
IBM Svenska AB, Via Piave 23, 31033 Castelfranco, Veneto, Italy
e-mail: alberto.pietrobon@se.ibm.com albertopt@gmail.com

M. Curley and P. Formica (eds.), *The Experimental Nature of New Venture Creation*, Innovation, Technology, and Knowledge Management, DOI: 10.1007/978-3-319-00179-1_10, © Springer International Publishing Switzerland 2013

Table 1 Demand and supply in the knowledge market

	The knowns (hold by brains)	The unknowns (not hold by brains)
Known (requested by would-be entrepreneurs)	Demand and supply exist	Demand exist supply does not exist
Unknown (not requested by would-be entrepreneurs)	Demand does not exist, supply exists	Demand and supply do not exist

A useful starting point in describing the knowledge market is a consideration of the factors that define the demand and supply variables: demand for knowledge comes from individuals who want to know more; the supply of knowledge is provided by experts who have the required information.

As in many other markets, demand and/or supply may or may not exist, in terms of what is not known and what is not known. Table 1 sets out the four possible combinations and relationships between demand and supply in the knowledge market. The 'known knowns' constitute all existing knowledge that experts can offer to would-be entrepreneurs. The 'known unknowns' are all those questions asked to which there is no current answer. The 'unknown knowns' are those topics on which information can be provided by experts, but for which there are no requests. The 'unknown unknowns' constitute knowledge that is neither requested nor available.

Is a scenario in which there is neither demand nor supply worth investigating? In a conventional market the fourth quadrant would be excluded a priori because it could never reach equilibrium; in contrast, in the knowledge market it represents the trigger for continuous improvement. Moreover, the fact that equilibrium can never be reached drives knowledge and innovation toward new frontiers. This is exactly what high-expectation entrepreneurs, whose aim is to make a major impact in the market, are constantly seeking; and this is what the experts, whose aim is to develop new knowledge continuously, can offer them. Both parties want to pursue unknown unknowns, since this is where strong competitive advantage may lie. This leads to our first question:

Q1: *In the knowledge market, is it possible for demand and supply to meet even in the context of unknown unknowns?*

Interpreting Simulation Outputs

Given that there is a way to connect high-expectation entrepreneurs to experts and thus that knowledge can move from one to the other, what is the potential for mutual understanding? Is it truly possible for nascent entrepreneurs and experts to communicate effectively so that each side fully comprehends the other's meaning and requirements?

This is a complex issue for both the demand and supply sides of the knowledge market. In the case of high-expectation entrepreneurs, it is often impossible for them to formulate a precise question as they are generally not sure what they are asking for. Moreover, if the questions are not clear, it will be difficult to establish whether the proposed solutions respond satisfactorily to the entrepreneurs' requests. As for the researchers and analysts on the supply side, the problems are largely the same. The unknown unknowns are constantly in the discovery phase: they are, by definition, not yet formalized and thus are very difficult to transmit. In other words, there is no certainty and everything is in a process of permanent change. This leads us to our second question:

Q2: *Can a high-expectation entrepreneur, travelling into the unknown unknowns, interpret the results of experiments in the right way?*

The Application of Learning

Assuming that high-expectation entrepreneurs do interpret correctly the unknown unknowns received from the experts, the next step is the practical application of the results of the academic simulation. How can would-be entrepreneurs put into practice a theoretical notion that has not been formalized? How can they make it useful for their start-up? Is it really possible to assume that, before launching a firm, high-expectation entrepreneurs can behave perfectly in accordance with a hypothesis formulated by others, even if the 'others' are experts in the field? More specifically, to what extent can high-expectation entrepreneurs apply to their businesses the interpretations of unknown unknowns provided by experts? Thus our third question is:

Q3: *How can would-be entrepreneurs be sure that they are learning how to behave effectively?*

A Premise to Further Analysis

In assessing a model that aims to reduce the risks of launching new start-ups, all dangers of misunderstanding must be addressed. The three questions itemized in the preceding section invite further reflection on what may be lacking, or as yet unexpressed, in the notion of experimental labs. The labs are the places where simulations occur; they are the virtual incubators that can transform intention into action. However, we also need to define the role of individuals in this model or, more specifically, the means of connecting two different groups of individuals (high-expectation entrepreneurs and experts).

Different kinds of ties need to be established, both weak and strong, to make the simulations work but, critically, an effective link is required before these ties can occur. This link, the linchpin, will be achieved by someone who can bridge the knowledge gap and enable connections between the two groups. Such a person, whom we shall call the 'venture-sitter', would be responsible for facilitating the exchange of knowledge. The term 'venture-sitter' is derived from 'baby-sitter': venture-sitters interact with entrepreneurial ideas (the 'children'), would-be entrepreneurs (the 'parents'), and with experts, who can be seen as the 'relatives' in this analogy. After gaining the trust of the potential entrepreneur and the experts, the venture-sitter continues to help the aspiring entrepreneurs by looking after their entrepreneurial ideas, nurturing them and encouraging their development in the best possible way, just as baby- sitters are expected to do with children.

The role of the knowledge exchange facilitator is very common in entrepreneurial studies. It is therefore important to underline here the main differences between venture-sitters and, for example, industrial liaison officers or incubator managers. All have crucial roles in knowledge transfer, but each has a specific function and performs it in a particular way—see Table 2, which shows that despite the initial similarities between the three roles there are in fact significant differences. Thus we will now define the specific role of the venture-sitter in more detail.

The Venture-Sitter

The critical importance of the role of the 'venture-sitter' becomes apparent when we examine the various achievable options regarding the creation of teams in the experimental business laboratory (lab) model. The final decision concerning the selection of the members of a lab who will work on a given start-up case can determine the success or failure of the business idea. The importance of the venture-sitter in this context can be demonstrated by a process of exclusion.

Table 2 Differences between industrial liaison officers, incubator managers, and venture-sitters

Industrial liaison officers	Incubator managers	Venture-sitters
Promote workshops, conferences, and events to develop entrepreneurial culture among researchers	Provide infrastructure to aspiring entrepreneurs to help them implement new ventures	Promote involvement in personal networks in order to test high-expectation ideas
Are interested in inventions and try to manage their licensing or patenting in order to create value	Are interested in businesses that meet the selective criteria of the incubator in order to create value	Are interested in experts who can improve the would-be entrepreneur's ideas in order to create value
Drive individual action, providing consulting, and administrative support	Drive individual action, providing physical spaces and/or furniture	Drive individual action, providing knowledge created by experts
Maintain a personal link with all the members in their sphere of influence	Supervise the incubating projects in order to evaluate them	Are members of the personal network around the would-be entrepreneur

First, it might be that all the lab members, having examined a particular case, take the ultimate decision of who will work on the new start-up project. In doing this, the members will carefully assess how their individual skills and expertise will match the case and will thus decide who will be best suited to take responsibility for the task. On the one hand, this process seems a sound one, in that it should produce the best fit between the high-expectation entrepreneur's needs and the experts' expertise. On the other hand, however, two practical impediments could arise. The first of these is time: the process would be very time-consuming and this works against the aim of reducing the 'time-to-market', a core aspect of the notion of the experimental lab. The second impediment relates to the number of members: the selection process will be increasingly difficult as the register of members increases.

Another possible approach would be the selection of appropriate project team members by the senior managers or directors of the lab. In this approach, the decision makers will mediate between the lab members and the would-be entrepreneur, addressing requests from both sides to create the best possible team. In practice, however, the lab managers will also be responsible for selecting and identifying new experts and enrolling them in the lab's network, so that the lab maintains a large number of available people and high level of knowledge. Thus the lab managers already have different tasks to fulfil and it may be too much to expect of them, in terms of the demands on their time, also to determine the membership of teams for new start-up projects. As mentioned previously, the main task concerns the interpretation and linkage of two different kinds of human capital: this requires people who are willing to dedicate a large amount of their individual time and resources to its accomplishment.

By a process of exclusion, therefore, the 'venture-sitter' may be the best option for creating teams in experimental business labs. The venture-sitter would be briefed by the lab's senior managers and would constitute the missing link between the lab's network of experts and the start-up idea. The venture-sitter would examine both the proposal of the high-expectation entrepreneur and the corresponding skills and expertise of the lab members and would then select the most suitable members for a given start-up.

All of this is necessary if the process of testing entrepreneurial ideas is to be both effective and as rapid as possible.

Team Creation

A further step in investigating the role of the venture- sitter is prompted by the fact that a lab's network will comprise a large number of experts, some of whom may belong to the same research field. Various questions thus arise. How will teams be formed? Who is going to join each experimental lab? And, since each aspect of the business could be handled by more than one expert, how many experts should be involved in a project?

In the following examples we take into account the various proposals concerning how experts are expected to work in an experimental lab. The experts may be experienced entrepreneurs, or may be based at universities, research centers, government or non- governmental organizations, venture capital firms, fund- raising bodies, or may have been previously involved in the supply chain, in consumer organizations, etc.

Option 1: A task force of experts works as a group.

In this first option all (or a number of) experts in a particular field will diagnose, analyze and make decisions by working as a group, constantly exchanging ideas, and reaching common conclusions (Fig. 1). This approach will make use of all the members' knowledge as well as creating ideas in a constant process of information exchange and feedback. However, it may be very time-consuming, for instance if the members are dispersed around the world. In addition, the coordination of these members within the time constraints that might apply for a project could prove difficult and challenging.

Option 2: A single member supervises a specific field.

Another approach would be to delegate the different fields of a start-up to only one member of the network, who will then be responsible for the decisions taken (Fig. 2). This process would be much faster in terms of information exchange and feedback between the venture-sitter and the lab members. However, in this case the knowledge that will be used will flow from only one selected person per field

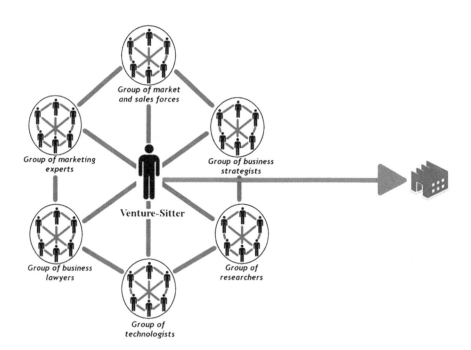

Fig. 1 A task force of experts will work in a group

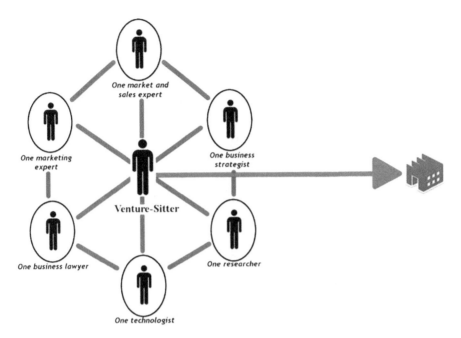

One market and
sales expert

One marketing
expert

One business
strategist

Venture-Sitter

One business lawyer

One researcher

One technologist

Fig. 2 Only one single member will supervise a specific field

and, even if he or she is an outstanding expert, experience suggests that group work always provides the best results.

Option 3: One member supervises a specific field, but communicates the outcome only after confirmation from all other members.

In this last alternative, there is still only one person with specific responsibility for each field relevant to the start-up proposal; but, before the findings are communicated to the venture-sitter, there has to be confirmation from all the other members specialized in their respective fields (Fig. 3). This approach is therefore a combination of the first two: the venture-sitter deals with only one member per field as in option 2, but any decision has to be approved by all the other members. In contrast to option 1, there will not be a continuous process of speculative, free-ranging thinking, discussion, and debate among members in the same field, but the final feedback will help to ensure that the ultimate decision is on the right track.

Conclusions

This chapter has focused on the role of the experts in the experimental laboratory approach to testing new business ideas. It has looked specifically at the creation of a 'venture-sitter' and the contribution that such a function could make to the

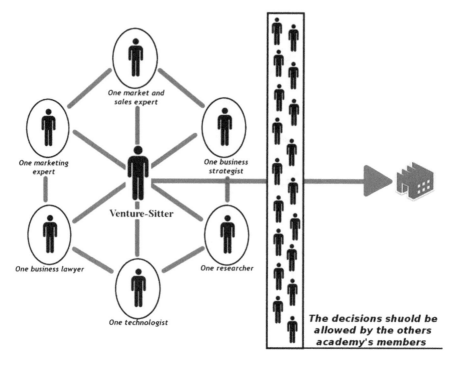

Fig. 3 Only one single member will supervise a specific field but will communicate the outcome only after a confirmation from all the other members

process. Further studies might investigate the characteristics of experts from two distinct perspectives. First, it is important to analyze the influence on one another of the experimental lab (that is, the range of assessment activities in practice) and the venture-sitter. The way an experimental business lab should work, with its distinctive features, requires specific individual characteristics on the part of the venture-sitter that, consequently, will reinforce the lab's distinctive approach and function. The second perspective will involve a comparison of different professional figures who, with their different backgrounds, participation, and contributions, could be of use in the launch of new ventures. Having set out the desirability and potential effectiveness of such a role, the precise nature and function of the venture-sitter certainly need to be accurately defined through a process of further reflection and analysis.

Part III
Practices of and for Experimentation

Chapter 11
Experimenting Social Constructivist Approach in Entrepreneurial Process-Based Training: Cases in Social, Creative and Technology Entrepreneurship

Tõnis Mets, Mervi Raudsaar and Kärt Summatavet

> *Entrepreneurship skills should be part of literacy—3rd literacy*
> *after reading and writing, and computer proficiency.*
> Anzori Barkalaja

Introduction

In this chapter, the authors deal with the social constructivist entrepreneurial process-based training methodology approach at venture creation across different fields as experienced by trainers moderating the learning process with both social entrepreneurs and technology entrepreneurs in traditional (handicraft) and virtual technologies. The social constructivist approach-based methodology was first developed for implementation within the framework of a venture lab-type of ecosystem/environment at the University of Tartu, Centre for Entrepreneurship.

T. Mets (✉) · M. Raudsaar
Centre for Entrepreneurship, University of Tartu, Ülikooli 18, 50090 Tartu, Estonia
e-mail: tonis.mets@ut.ee

M. Raudsaar
Soinaste 41A, 50404 Tartu, Estonia
e-mail: mervi.raudsaar@ut.ee

T. Mets
Ratsu tee 14, Kakumetsa, Luunja vald, 62203 Tartumaa, Estonia

K. Summatavet
Estonian Academy of Arts, Haaviku tee 1A, 10143 Tallinn, Estonia
e-mail: kart@kiirtee.ee

Haaviku tee 1A, 12113 Tallinn, Estonia

M. Curley and P. Formica (eds.), *The Experimental Nature of New Venture Creation*,
Innovation, Technology, and Knowledge Management, DOI: 10.1007/978-3-319-00179-1_11,
© Springer International Publishing Switzerland 2013

The combination of the above methodology with the venture lab environment was called Entrepreneurship Home® and registered as the trademark of the University of Tartu. Following this, the Entrepreneurship Home® methodology was incorporated into mainstream entrepreneurship courses across study programs of the university, including adult training courses.

The theoretical background of the method uses aspects of several theories:

- Social Constructive Learning concept;
- Humanistic Learning concept and
- Co-operative Learning.

The Entrepreneurship Home® model of learning combines these theories and applies them to its own learning environment, where one goal is to help students develop as entrepreneurs and marketing professionals. The learning process aims to be as realistic as possible following the entrepreneurial process from self-actualisation of entrepreneurship to opportunity recognition, venture launch and business development, and consists of three main methods:

- Learning by doing;
- Kolb's learning cycle and
- Dialogue.

Learning by doing and Kolb's learning cycle are quite close to problem-based learning methods, where students learn by applying the subject to be learnt to practical problems. After recognising a problem, the students look for potential solutions and then evaluate the impacts of those solutions. While implementing their projects, the students use textbooks and other sources, and previous experiences of their own, or those of other teams to find solutions to the challenges and problems they encounter.

Our goal was through training, learning and venture creation experiments to comparatively test the applicability of the Entrepreneurship Home® methodology for venture creation in different fields of entrepreneurship.

Implementation of the Entrepreneurship Home® methodology and new venture creation took place across three different partly overlapping fields:

- Social or community entrepreneurship;
- Entrepreneurship in creative industries (handicraft) or creative entrepreneurship and
- Internet-based or virtual (sports coaching) business.

The venture creation experiments in these three fields are described by three different case studies. The Non-profit Lahemaa Craft Workshop and business venture Swift Hand cases were created within the framework of the adult training project "Handicraft for Job 2", whereas the case Sportlyzer was an outcome of the part-time student's study program. The cases were experiments not only for the founders of these new ventures, but also for the trainers. Indeed, in addition to the three business case studies, the current chapter is in itself a case study of

Entrepreneurship Home® and the processes leading to venture creation within that environment which have experiential character.

Before describing the main methodological aspects of the training and learning processes, and the cases, first, a general introduction into the constructivist approach within the Entrepreneurship Home® will be given in the next section, followed by some particular aspects of the concrete fields of cases studied. Research tasks related to the cases were the identification of key aspects of the entrepreneurial process and the experiential character of venture creation.

Theoretical Background of Learning in the Entrepreneurship Home®

Entrepreneurship training environment Entrepreneurship Home® is based on experiential learning theory integrated with social constructive, humanistic and co-operative learning concepts. David A. Kolb's Experiential Learning Theory (ELT) defines learning as the process whereby knowledge is created through the transformation of experience, whereby knowledge results from the combination of grasping and transforming experience (Kolb 1984). ELT as defined by Kolb posits that learning is the major determinant of human development and how individuals learn shapes the course of their personal development.

The Social Constructive Learning concept (Dewey 2009; Vygotskii 1978) focuses on uncovering the ways in which individuals and groups participate in the creation of their perceived social reality. Socially constructed reality is seen as an ongoing, dynamic process. Reality is reproduced by people acting on their interpretations and their knowledge of it. The term describes the way learners construct their reality and learning through selecting and interpreting, through previous experiences and through the feedback they receive on their work. Learning is therefore context-oriented. The social environment, working with others, is an especially important factor in this process.

The Humanistic Learning concept (Rogers and Freiberg 1994; Knowles 1990) emphasises learning as an individual process. Learning is based on the experiences of the learner and their ability to reflect these experiences. Learning is also seen as an inborn human quality, a need that every human being must satisfy after the basic needs (according to Maslow's theory) have been satisfied. Teachers should support the growth and the special potential of each individual learner.

The Co-operative Learning (Johnson and Johnson 1999) method involves the positive interdependence of learners: the success of an individual depends on the success of the team. In this approach, individual responsibility for the result is required including support to the higher competence of teamwork and group decision making, and rejection of ineffective working methods.

The theoretical approach "learning by doing" was created by American teacher John Dewey (1859–1952), father of the experimental educational movement. His educational philosophy had two underlying basic assumptions:

- throughout one's whole life mental development and growth is ongoing, and
- any kind of human life is social by its nature (Dewey 2009).

Another central notion in Dewey's philosophical context is experience. This can be physical, psychical or mental and it is both a device for assisting education and the objective of education. The coach (master) has to offer experiences for the learner (apprentice) which are associated with earlier experiences the apprentice may have. These experiences are provided by sensual perceptions and become, through logical thinking, explicative devices for an individual. But direct transfer of experiences to apprentices is relatively impossible; their recognition should be achieved via reciprocal impact of action and environment (ibid).

Kolb's learning cycle is based on John Dewey's claim that learning must be grounded in experience, Lewin's (1951) ideas of the importance of active learning, and Piaget's (1966) emphasis on the interaction between person and environment on intelligence (Fig. 1) (Kolb 1984; Cobb and Yaeckel 1996). The approach demonstrates that most learning processes are based on specific actions yielding

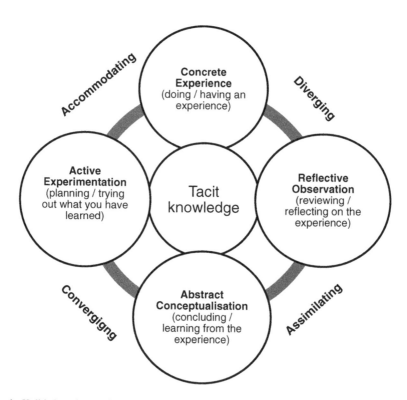

Fig. 1 Kolb's learning cycle. *Source* based on Kolb (1984)

experiences comprising the results of those actions in the specific situation (Kolb et al. 2000).

Another reason for the attractiveness of this model in entrepreneurship education is Kolb's emphasis on the cycle spiral: it is often necessary to go through the four stages several times in order to fully understand the general principles; in this way the learning process can be adopted by people with differing learning styles.

In order to develop thinking and practical professional skills, it is not, however, sufficient to plan, do, evaluate and re-plan. It is also necessary that the tacit knowledge that the learners gain and possess is exchanged and shared. This takes place through dialogue.

New things and learning situations generate new ideas and provide the learner with new viewpoints for looking back at old issues. These ideas can be transformed into practical activity and plans that are realised in life, while within these plans individual thoughts are put onto paper thus making them concrete. After this, experiments are made, testing how the plan works in practice. When the experiment has been carried out, e.g. in the form of a development project, its successes and failures generate personal experiences of those things that work and those that do not. These experiences then form a basis for new learning situations and events and generate more thoughts. Ideas, their realisation, experiments and experiences form a cycle of learning that keeps feeding itself and enables learning by doing.

Entrepreneurship Home® as Laboratory of Venture Creation

The theoretical framework for Entrepreneurship Home® in addition to the learning concepts highlighted above is much wider and includes the whole entrepreneurial process with its phases/stages from idea generation to exit from the business, resources, knowledge environment and knowledge transfer, and feedback on decision making, etc. However, we can enlighten only some of those factors which surround the venture creation process.

Training has a central role in developing a trainee's entrepreneurial personality and a coach is a person who leads and controls the realisation of the goals of the trainee. A coach is a modern leader whose status is not based on power and authority. While a coach belongs within a learners' team, more than anything he or she operates at an individual level, taking responsibility for the development of the entire community, as well.

Effective recognition of opportunities is considered one of the most important outcomes of entrepreneurial learning in an experiential process (Politis 2005). From the perspective of entrepreneurial learning (ibid), it is more or less an individual process. But organisational learning of SMEs in terms of an entrepreneur's capacity to learn and to integrate the working team remains the leading factor; and entrepreneurial learning is mostly an action-learning process (Deakins et al. 2000).

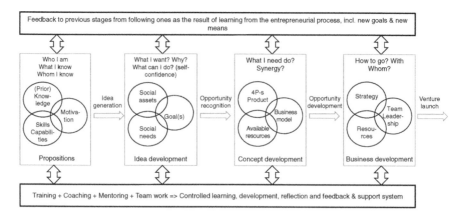

Fig. 2 Entrepreneurial process-based learning and venture creation model and environment Entrepreneurship Home®

This process is not linear as could be seen from the cyclic character of learning according to Kolb (1984), and in the entrepreneurial process it needs to alternately adapt means and goals (Sarasvathy 2008) to realise the idea. The venture creation process described in Fig. 2 in the context of training is an iterative, nonlinear, feedback-driven, conceptual and physical process that reflects the venture creation process as it happens in real life.

The training process in Fig. 2 follows the logic of entrepreneurial process as previously described by a number of authors (Davidsson 2005; Sarasvathy et al. 2005) and includes the following sub-processes/stages/actions: Idea generation, Opportunity recognition, Opportunity development and Venture launch with different levels of differentiation of stages. Venture launch could also be understood as opportunity exploitation. Propositions and outcomes of the entrepreneurial process and its single sub-processes are somehow mentally and physically embedded in the entrepreneur (or team) and the venture creation environment (prior to the venture launch).

The concept of silo is used here to label the combination of physical and mental shapes corresponding to a single stage. That means embedding propositions, outcomes and other mental and physical means of sub-processes in silos Propositions, Idea development, Concept development and Business development driven/controlled by direct (entrepreneurial) processes of venture creation as well as by the feedback chain.

Feedback signals/information of any mismatch here necessitates a change in the content of silos (models) and a new iteration, involving all actions/stages or parts of them—which may take place as described by Kolb (1984), or a new combination of goals and means leads the process as suggested by Sarasvathy (2008) and embeds in the silos again. The content of a silo is not static; components of it are in reciprocal interaction as well as in interaction with the main entrepreneurial process. Sometimes, as a result of learning from the process there is a need for a change of initial idea or business concept as shown with feedback arrows in Fig. 2—the training process in the Entrepreneurship Home®. All the entrepreneurial learning processes are supported by the staff of the Centre for Entrepreneurship and this includes provision of training, coaching, mentoring and team facilitation, and has extended to providing work space for newly launched businesses.

Propositions. Among propositions, individual motivational and cognitive aspects affect entrepreneurial processes as seen by Kickul et al. (2009) while Shane (2000) focuses on prior knowledge and experience necessary for successful opportunity recognition. Frequently, the origin of a new venture idea derives from an entrepreneurs' own background (education, work experience, hobby, family tradition, etc.), sometimes called pre-history (Mets 2009, 2012).

Idea development. Personal experience can be a valuable source of new venture ideas, but the idea must meet consumers' needs—therefore "social needs" can be understood as the gaps between desirable situation and reality in business as well in social entrepreneurship (Guclu et al. 2002). In both fields social assets, such as attitude, desire for healthy lifestyle or tradition, which can be embedded in people, communities or networks are supportive of the launch of new ideas, services or products. Plausible evaluation of social needs and social assets is the basis for feasible idea development and realistic, but motivating goal setting which leads to opportunity recognition.

Concept development. While there usually exists a wide range of opportunities—"opportunity window", what can be developed depends upon the available resources and means, product/service and related marketing-mix. A good business model will combine in the best way marketing, capabilities and different company resources to enable further development opportunities and by happy coincidence can create synergistic effects that competitors do not possess. At this stage it is also possible to test the market for the product: customers can be involved in product and business model development via socialisation with co-learners, participation in fairs or launching a Beta-version of an Internet product.

Business development. This is the stage for preparing the venture to become real, to be launched. That means formulation of strategy, acquiring any missing tangible and intangible resources, and teambuilding, but also dealing with any remaining legal issues prior to launching the venture. Although the company can be legally created some preparations for product launch and entering the market may not yet be completed. Sometimes, besides venture growth, new product development is the second best strategy for high-tech venture that enables a later exit by an entrepreneur.

Although timing of some specific events within venture creation can be defined very exactly, e.g. legal registration, then due to the iterative creation process, venture development can be positioned across different stages even independently of legal requirements. However, the initial idea generation and launch of the venture can be identified somewhat more precisely than other stages. In the Entrepreneurship Home® the student/trainee usually starts his or her entrepreneurial process from inception—i.e. propositions, but collaboration network can be much wider just as it is in real life.

Where the Ideas and Motivation Come from: Linking Prior and New Knowledge into Entrepreneurial Process

Even if the students/trainees coming to Entrepreneurship Home® have not yet identified their venture idea this does not mean that the opportunity they discover is absolutely new for them. Research among active technology entrepreneurs by Shane (2000) demonstrated that individuals discover opportunities related to their prior knowledge. Shaver and Scott (1991), and Kickul et al. (2009) revealed the significant role of the person, especially his/her distinct cognitive style as a determinant of success in the different stages of the new venture creation process. Individuals with the intuitive cognitive style can be more confident in identifying and recognising opportunities than individuals with the analytic cognitive style (Kickul et al. 2009). High-tech entrepreneurship has been quite a popular target for research and we have quite a lot of information about the origin of prior knowledge in this field (e.g. Shane 2000), but we know less about handicraft, which can also be considered as a specific field of technology as well as creative industry.

Personal experience and inherited skills tacitly lie in the minds of another target group, as Niedderer and Imani (2008) suggest, in regard to Michael Polanyi's explanation that tacit knowledge is the "personal coefficient" part of any explicit knowledge. They propose that the experiential and procedural knowledge (learning by doing) have both explicit and tacit dimensions. The experience can be named and its quality indicatively described, but the essence of this experience cannot be communicated and therefore any interpretation of the experience remains grounded in 'tacit knowledge' (Niedderer and Imani 2008). Many current academic debates on knowledge management and innovation management of experiential knowledge and reflective practice in the field of art and design (see for example Schön 1983; Nonaka et al. 2000; Biggs 2004; Scrivener 2006) contribute to devise a framework for building coherent and rigorous methodologies for research in the creative and practice-based disciplines. However, in our case study we aimed to activate trainees' creative imagination in finding new product development or service ideas on the basis of their personal experience and tacit knowledge. Product ideas born from local culture and family traditions, inherited skills (those passed on from previous generations) and shared knowledge of the local community gave great joy to their creators and also captivated various consumer and client groups.

According to Storkerson (2009), "experiential knowledge and thinking focus on the contextualised or situated, ecological, level everyday existence as it unfolds to an actor, rather than on structured argument that is schematized, enclosed and defined from outside". Experiential knowing is intuitive. However, Niedderer and Imani argue that Knowledge Management has problematized individual tacit knowledge and social tacit knowledge by aiming to offer ways in which they can be captured or 'converted' into explicit knowledge (Niedderer and Imani 2008). In relation to the SECI model of Ikujiro Nonaka's knowledge conversion theory (Nonaka et al. 2000), they propose that explicit and tacit knowledge are different dimensions of a unified concept of knowledge. All knowledge has an explicit dimension that can be communicated by conventional means, but cannot fully convey the tacit dimension of knowledge. The tacit dimension of knowledge is ineffable and it cannot be converted into explicit knowledge. In order to share it, it has to be transferred or evoked in other ways in its tacit form (Niedderer and Imani 2008).

However, Guclu et al. emphasise that ideas commonly have their roots in the personal experience of the entrepreneur, but recognising social needs, social assets and change can also lead to the generation of promising ideas (Guclu et al. 2002). They argue that for social entrepreneurs, an "attractive" opportunity is one that has sufficient potential for positive social impact to justify the investment of time, energy and money required to pursue it seriously (ibid). Innovative ideas can be generated systematically, but at the same time, converting a promising idea into a workable and attractive opportunity requires an on-going creative process working hand-in-hand with focused analysis, experimentation and sometimes even launching the initial stages of a venture. They argue that social entrepreneurs add the most significant value in this stage of the process, and few promising ideas make it through the development funnel to become opportunities worth pursuing in the long term (ibid).

Empirical Research and Methodology

This study's design was guided by our aim to explore entrepreneurial process-based entrepreneurship learning, and the venture creation model (as a process), prior knowledge and/or (traditional/inherited) handicrafts (as an object) and exploitation of local/global resources in building a new venture in the field of hi-tech, handicraft and community entrepreneurship (as an environment). We focus on experimental process-based entrepreneurship teaching (as in Fig. 2), in order to explain how the skills, knowledge and attitudes develop in individual, group and society levels and how networking becomes an effective training method for encouraging co-operation inside the community during the three-year project period.

Therefore our approach is very much process based. Our starting point has been that entrepreneurial teaching is not only effective on a theoretical basis, since this is not just about transferring novel knowledge but also involves discovering and activating the knowledge a subject already possesses; all this should take place in a holistic context (both process, object, tacit knowledge and environment are considered).

We tested this assumption according to the original venture creation model (Fig. 2) which was our first opportunity to implement that model in both training and venture creation research—in this respect the overall process was experimental. We thus have available three case studies of experimental venture creation processes in the framework of pilot project "Handicraft for Job 2" and a regular part-time master program in Entrepreneurship and Technology Management at the University of Tartu. The empirical part of this chapter uses qualitative methods, more specifically phenomenology and case studies. Phenomenology enables us to describe the meaning and impact of particular experience on the people involved—and offer the specific mapping of it. Such an individual description is used for deriving more common and universal meanings, in other words the structural core of an experience (Creswell 1998).

At the same time, the qualitative phenomenological method is rather revealing while describing individual experience on cognition of some social actor or relation: in other words, phenomenon—how this is realised, interpreted and later applied in social practices (Rossman and Rallis 1998). In our case, we search for answers as to how experimental learning helped participants to reach the point of creating a new venture. We discuss what aspects and conditions enabled an effective outcome for the pilot project "Handicraft for Job 2" and what were the roles of networking, community creation, product development and mentoring in the learning process and results.

Thus, we studied how counterparts of the studying process describe the genesis of their venture idea, from its creation up to implementation, i.e. establishment of the company.

The qualitative method is therefore an especially fruitful research procedure since there is need to study the entire ecosystem of learning and how participants perceive process-based learning. Another reason why the qualitative method was chosen by the authors is its suitability to extract information from personal experiences and opinions that is difficult to access using quantitative methods.

The subjects of the research were participants undertaking entrepreneurial training to create their own business venture. The participants understanding of the enterprise development process would enable the researchers to investigate how the process-based entrepreneurial study and ecosystem can assist people's decision making when creating a new venture and its features.

Case studies based on secondary data and personal interviews were used for mapping the main factors of the experiential learning process (as shown in Fig. 2) which lead the trainee to creating a new venture. First the authors' own observation and knowledge are used; second a search of online publications was carried out using Google. After that, web pages and annual reports of the companies were studied. The data collected were evaluated in the context of entrepreneurial process; aspects not covered previously and newer trends were mapped, while some interpretations were cross-checked during interviews.

Three Cases of Experimental Venture Creation

Cases in the current chapter are presented in Table 1 according to the research questions determined for mapping the entrepreneurial process (as in Fig. 2) of different ventures. The facts shown in Table 1 are presented very concisely in note form, but disclosed in more detail in the section on findings and discussion.

Table 1 Experimental cases of venture creation in the Entrepreneurship Home®

Company name; founders; founding data	Sportlayzer; Jüri Kaljundi, Tõnis Saag; 09.07.2009; private limited company	Swift Hand; Kati Kibena; 27.07.2010; private limited company	Lahemaa craft workshop; Marit Oinus; 16.11.2010; non-profit venture
Propositions: pre-history			
Prior experience in entrepreneurship of founder(s)	Yes, founders of OÜ VOMAX, CV-Online; social media start-up www.nagi.ee, etc.	Has been sole proprietor	No
Prior experiences and skills in the area(s)	Sports/coaching—karate champion; web-business; social media	Has learned and worked as seamstress	Has learned special pedagogy and handicraft
Prior knowledge of product, service and technology	Sports/coaching; software development; social media	Professional seamstress, local traditional handicraft skills, professional shop assistant	Art therapist; local traditional handicraft skills
Prior networks	Internet social media; personal network in (hobby) sports	No	Ecological community
Where did the idea come from?	From own personal background and networking	From own personal background; specific idea came following a study visit to the Estonian National Museum	In connection with her background and new place of home
Idea development			
Social needs; target group	Healthy sports lifestyle, individual coaching for active busy people; "white collar workers"	Original and individual products; consumers interested in local lifestyle, cultural tourists, local community	Creativity centre; community development. "Eco" and "ethno" people; young generation and people with special needs
Social assets	Awareness of healthy lifestyle, social media	Awareness of original and individual lifestyle	Awareness of eco-friendly lifestyle and culture; local community development incl. special program for people with special needs
Goal	Virtual individual non-expensive sports coach for everybody, healthy lifestyle	Offering individual, culturally original clothing style, ethno trend	Cultural entertainment for visitors and members of workshops

(continued)

Table 1 (continued)

	Sportlayzer; Jüri Kaljundi, Tõnis Saag; 09.07.2009; private limited company	Swift Hand; Kati Kibena; 27.07.2010; private limited company	Lahemaa craft workshop; Marit Oinus; 16.11.2010; non-profit venture
Company name; founders; founding data			
Market orientation (domestic/ International)	International/global	Domestic/international	Domestic/international (cultural tourists)
Concept development			
Business model (BM)	Freemium BM, *for free* service creates synergy by involving customer in early stages of business development	Simple BM	Collaboration of nature and culture reserve inhabitants' community for cultural tourism
Product/service	Virtual individual sports coach for hobby sport-people	New trend of local clothes of linen for children and adults, opening a studio of custom sewing	Special workshops and events based on values embedded in local culture and ecological lifestyle; ceramics
Market and target group; Accessibility	Global; Active people with healthy lifestyle; Virtual free reach everywhere	Domestic/international Consumers interested in local lifestyle, cultural tourists, local community. Own studio and shop; special tourist markets, malls, webpage	Domestic/international (cultural tourists). "Eco" and "ethno" people; young generation and people with special needs. Social capital and networks. Local municipality and community; the state museum's shop
Promotion	Supported by business model and social media	Social media; fairs	Social network
Price	Basic product for free, low price compared to live personal coach	Appropriate price calculated by amount of work, quality of natural materials and handiwork	Through negotiation with customers
Available resources	Experience of professional and hobby sportsmen tracked as a free contribution of customers into product and business model development Seed and venture capital	Agreements with different suppliers	Her unique place of home. Social and community network. Some project-based financing

(continued)

Table 1 (continued)

	Sportlayzer; Jüri Kaljundi, Tõnis Saag; 09.07.2009; private limited company	Swift Hand; Kati Kibena; 27.07.2010; private limited company	Lahemaa craft workshop; Marit Oinus; 16.11.2010; non-profit venture
Company name; founders; founding data			
Business development			
Leadership; team/employees (incl. founders)	8, team: team leader and coach, marketing and web consulting, sports psychologist, researcher, interface designers, software engineer, marketing manager	1 (owner)	1 (one of the founders), community members on sub-contracting basis
Strategy	Involvement of customers into business development via freemium BM	Involvement of customers into business development via needs and feedback	Community's needs and feedback
Product development strategy	Virtual personal coach, Launched for tests 22/03/2011, for free	High quality of ideas, products and materials	Attractive content of workshops and ventures
Resources: intangible and tangible	Intangible: unique combination of competencies of inter-disciplinary team	Intangible: unique and attractive design; tangible: high quality of materials and handiwork	Intangible: ecological approach, re-use and development of local traditions and practices according to community's social and cultural needs. Tangible: attractive environment
Financial resources, support	Estonian Development Fund, private investors	Labour Market Board	Self-financed and project-based EU funding
Venture launch			
When started?	During studies for master program Entrepreneurship and Technology Management, 2009	Immediately after finishing the project Handicraft for Job 2 and getting grant, 2010	During the project Handicraft for Job 2, 2010
Where started?	Location: Tartu Science Park. Web launched	Location: Tartu	Location: own farm in Lahemaa National Park
Plans for expanding	Global market	Not at the moment	Not at the moment

Sources Estonian Development Fund (2010); Kibena (2012); Oinus (2012); Sportlyzer (2010), (2012)

Findings and Discussion About Venture Creation in Different Fields of Entrepreneurship

Although one of the authors, Tõnis Mets, has used the general schema of entrepreneurial process-based training for venture creation since 1994 (following his own entrepreneurial experience and learning from Swedish trainers), the Entrepreneurship Home® concept was shaped into the current theoretical framework and methodology form after his visit to the centre for entrepreneurship of young people "Intotalo" in Kajaani, Finland in 2006. During 2007 a team of trainers from the University of Tartu learned more about the roots of "Intotalo" training methodology visiting Tiimiakatemia (Team Academy), which is the Entrepreneurship Centre of Excellence of the JAMK University of Applied Sciences in Jyväskylä, Finland.

The essence of this experience has been described in Fig. 2, the entrepreneurial process-based training in the Entrepreneurship Home® environment, and represents the underlying basis for analysing case studies and composing conclusions for this article. The cases followed phases of process-based training as shown in Fig. 2 and it became possible to map all phases in the context of three case studies through this research. An essential component of the process was training sessions of one or two days with breaks of several weeks to allow for the implementation the results of session and preparation for the following session. It became obvious that the Entrepreneurship Home® approach is valid across the spheres of several different activities: our case studies included new (high) technology, (inherited/traditional) handicrafts and community entrepreneurship.

New entrepreneurial propositions and ideas are not created into a void environment but they are supported by an entrepreneur's earlier experiences and particular social needs. The key factors are prior knowledge, skills, capabilities and motivation, which have a direct impact on the novelty, essential quality and consequences of the new enterprise. Our case studies show that immediate or concrete experiences are the basis for observations and reflections that can be actively tested and would serve as guides in creating new experiences and new ventures.

During the training process an entrepreneur should become conscious and adequately assess his/her personal capabilities, in order to be creative in combining personal cognitive experiences to expectations and social needs of their own venture's target groups. The feedback by their co-learners' group and coaches enables them to test and develop their ideas for a new enterprise and satisfying market expectations.

Differences and similarities of the four venture creation phases in Fig. 2 were identified:

Propositions describe personal traits and prior knowledge and experiences of nascent entrepreneurs. According to our cases, all entrepreneurs exploited their earlier knowledge and experiences; sometimes this was done in part unconsciously, as demonstrated below.

The experimental learning process of an entrepreneur opens new possibilities for them (as adult learners) to discover and evaluate their tacit knowledge and skills. They can then engage these purposely and creatively in finding new enterprise and attractive ideas, suited to customers needs and market demands. Co-founder and CEO of Sportlayser Tõnis Saag was encouraged by his hobbies and lifestyle, his own network helped him find a business partner sharing his views.

Kati Kibena, being tired of her previous job, was very confident that she would definitely not establish a new venture in the field she has been studying and worked for a long period. However, in reality she became inspired by the creative learning environment of Entrepreneurship Home®, which gave a new start to her professional life. Her new design of a unique linen clothes' collection, the result of her product development studies, became the core for a new venture.

Similarly, another entrepreneur, Marit Oinus, was seeking to change her lifestyle by moving from the capital city to a nature reserve. There she met a much wider interest in ecological tourism among the local community around her new home. Her educational and earlier work experience found a new application.

As we can see, a coach's support for a trainee's self-analysis and self-actualisation of their own skills and knowledge has the utmost importance. The major engaging motivator of all three cases has been self-realisation and mission rather than earning profit.

Idea development. Social assets and needs were at the disposal of the entrepreneur. These aspects have been considered most important in the context of social entrepreneurship, but as demonstrated by Sportlyzer their business idea targeted to healthy lifestyle has a deep social dimension as well. Our cases reveal that entrepreneurs take these aspects into consideration across all areas of their activities and the resulting analyses guarantee more structured and better stated target objectives. As a consequence, their ventures are more likely to meet the expectations of their communities wherever they are located—locally or globally. An additional positive factor is the enhancement of product idea by involving group members and coaches.

Concept development. testing the product or service among customers and receiving their feedback. In the case of Swift Hand (Kati Kibena), the communication with customers took place at fairs and it appeared to be very useful. Later on, as her characteristic style developed, she became more selective concerning feedback.

In the case of Craft Workshop (Marit Oinus), the actual service testing also took place during the concept development stage and this helped to more adequately describe the business model and demonstrated that instead of providing all cultural and arts training herself, it would be reasonable to collaborate with members of the local community through offering some combined services with them. Of course, some training, directed towards the community or specific target groups are still offered by Marit herself. The business model of the non-profit organisation was chosen since it appeared to be most effective way to attract additional investments.

Creation of the freemium business model for Sportlyzer (Tõnis Saag) gained much inspiration from the experience of the Skype globalisation, starting from a single worldwide free product, but following global breakthrough leveraging with a wider range of improvements and additional premium (paid) functionality. Sportlizer did even more, based on a Beta-version of the Internet product;

using the freemium business model and social media their customers are actively involved into product (concept) development, which can be called a Living Lab environment.

Business development. It is significant that two of the three entrepreneurs did not reveal any signs of moving towards foreign markets during the initial phase. However, through answers to questioning it became obvious that Swift Hand had been trying to get contacts from other countries and develop sales there (visiting fairs). Craft Workshop had tourists interested in culture as one of their target groups. In fact, both entrepreneurs actually would have liked to expand abroad but were afraid of making this decision (being back in the beginning of development spiral as they were in the beginning of creating their venture—and they were waiting for significant impact to verbalise their objective and hints for actions). But Sportlyzer using the freemium business model acknowledged that domestic or even a neighbouring foreign market is insufficient for them. Their teambuilding was very significant in gathering together an inter- and multi-disciplinary team for creating virtual intelligent consultancy in sports coaching for active people worldwide.

The ideas for new ventures created by the social entrepreneurs in our case study rely mainly on local culture, tradition and education, intertwined with personal experiential knowledge and creativity. The creative process of a specific promising idea and the launch of a new venture is developed thoroughly during the experiential learning process, and is highly influenced by the background of each individuals' education and specialisation. In our case studies, the shared values of the traditional community also functioned as a source of inspiration for personal experimentation in combining traditional inherited skills with the needs of modern society.

When characterising the venture creation process according to Fig. 2 using the three cases as examples, it becomes clear that this is not some kind of closed or isolated phenomenon but integrated with support from national, European or worldwide networks. Swift Hand and Craft Workshop gained much additional process stimulation from the product development and study visit programs in addition to the main training course. "Sportlyzer has passed through the international business incubator of the Development Fund, the SeedBooster, where the business plan and realisation tactics were polished up to clear goals and milestones" (Estonian Development Fund 2010).

The most significant value of the experiential learning process has been creation of new ventures that inspires the social entrepreneurs' imagination and empathy, and encourages them to implement both implicit and explicit resources of the (local and global) community. We argue that social entrepreneurs offer many diverse and novel ideas on how local traditional culture can be captured or converted into explicit knowledge and new values through creating a new venture that may offer a change of lifestyle and well-being for the local community. A pure business idea through its venturing model can turn into a social contribution to the global community for a healthy lifestyle as seen above.

Thus, an even higher efficiency can be achieved through entrepreneurial process-based training in the Entrepreneurship Home® environment, if other simultaneous training has a supportive character. It is clear that the training process does not cease with the formal completion of entrepreneurial process-based training, but continues through the community and teamwork created during the venture creation process. This implies that while the Entrepreneurship Home® has a significant place in the framework for training/learning process in the course of venture creation, the balance turns very quickly in favour of the entrepreneur as an adult learner.

Conclusions

Three experimental cases of venture creation in the entrepreneurial process-based learning framework Entrepreneurship Home® within the current research prove our earlier understanding that new venture ideas are the result of creative experiential learning process based on entrepreneur's prior knowledge and specific social needs. In our study in the field of hi-tech, handicraft and social/community entrepreneurship, prior knowledge, skills and capabilities and motivation had a key role in that process through influences on the novelty, quality and performance of the new venture, independently of the field of activities. Our case studies show that immediate or concrete experiences are the basis for observations and reflections that can be actively tested and serve as guides in creating new experiences and new ventures.

The special role of the learning community in the training process as well as the company's own team and social community should be mentioned for all three case ventures. But even more importantly, the case companies although from different fields followed similar patterns according to the original model of (training) venture creation compiled for the current research. Of course, there is still the need to elaborate further the concepts and models, and their combinations underling each of the stages or sub-processes of the entrepreneurial process, here defined as the content of special silos. Questions are open about whether the concept of silo is the most appropriate, or do we need some alternative concept description such as ba space as proposed by Nonaka et al. (2000) in knowledge management. Our research points to new challenges in understanding entrepreneurial new venture creation processes.

Acknowledgements The authors acknowledge the support offered by the Estonian Ministry of Education's project SF 0180037s08 and CB INTERREG IVA projects CREAENT and ENTREINT, and ESF HRD Programme Measure 1.3.1 project No. 1.3.0102.09-0036 "Handicraft for Job 2".

References

Biggs, M. A. R. (2004). Learning from experience: approaches to the experiential component of practice-based research. In H. Karlsson (Ed.), *Forskning, Reflektion, Utveckling* (pp. 6–21). Stockholm: Vetenskapsrådet.

Cobb, P., & Yaeckel, E. (1996). Constructivist, emergent and sociocultural perspectives in the context of developmental research. *Educational Psychologist, 31*(3/4), 175–190.

Creswell, J. W. (1998). *Qualitative inquiry and research design: Choosing among five traditions.* London: Sage Publications.

Davidsson, P. (2005). The entrepreneurial process as a matching problem, *Academy of Management Conference, Hawaii,* 5–10 August. Retrieved July 21, 2012, from http://eprints. qut.edu.au/archive/00002064/.

Deakins, D., O'Neill, E., & Mileham, P. (2000). Executive learning in entrepreneurial firms and the role of external directors. *Education + Training, 42*(4/5), 317–325.

Dewey, J. (2009). *Democracy and education: An introduction to the philosophy of education.* New York: WLC Books. (Original work published 1916).

Estonian Development Fund (2010, September 01). Development fund steps in with investment in earlier phase than before. *News,* Retrieved July 21, 2012, from http://www.arengufond.ee/e ngnews/investment/news1758/.

Guclu, A., Dees, J., & Anderson, B. B. (2002). *The process of social entrepreneurship: Creating opportunities worthy of serious pursuit.* CASE Working Paper Series 3, Center for the Advancement of Social Entrepreneurship, Duke University, Durham.

Johnson, D. W., & Johnson, R. T. (1999). Making cooperative learning work. *Theory into Practice, 38*(2), 67–73.

Kibena, K. (2012). Interview, by Raudsaar, M., June 28.

Kickul, J., Gundry, L. K., Barbosa, S. D., & Whitcanack, L. (2009). Intuition versus analysis? Testing differential models of cognitive style on entrepreneurial self-efficacy and the new venture creation process, *Entrepreneurship Theory and Practice, 33,* 439–453.

Knowles, M. S. (1990). The adult learner: a neglected species (4th ed.). Houston: Gulf Publishing.

Kolb, D. A. (1984). *Experiential learning: experience as the source of learning and development.* New Jersey: Prentice-Hall.

Kolb, D. A., Boyatzis, R., & Mainemelis, C. (2000). Experiential learning theory: previous research and new directions. In R. J. Sternberg & L. F. Zhang (Eds.), *Perspectives on cognitive, learning, and thinking styles.* New Jersey: Lawrence Erlbaum.

Lewin, K. (1951). *Field theory in social science.* New York: Harper & Row.

Mets, T. (2009). Creating global business model for knowledge-intensive SMEs: The small transition country cases. *Economics and Management, 14,* 466–475.

Mets, T. (2012). Creative business model innovation for globalizing SMEs. In T. Burger-Helmchen (Ed.), *Entrepreneurship: Creativity and Innovative Business Models.* Rijeka: InTech. Retrieved from: http://www.intechopen.com/books/entrepreneurship-creativity-and-innovative-business-mod els/creative-business-model-innovation-for-globalizing-smes.

Niedderer, K. & Imani, Y. (2008). Developing a framework for managing tacit knowledge in research using knowledge management models. In *Undisciplined! Proceedings of the Design Research Society Conference* 2008. Sheffield: Sheffield Hallam University.

Nonaka, I., Toyama, R., & Konno, N. (2000). SECI, ba, and leadership: a unified model of dynamic knowledge creation. *Long Range Planning, 33*(1), 5–34.

Oinus, M. (2012) Interview, by Raudsaar, M., June 15.

Piaget, J. (1966). *Psychology of intelligence.* Totowa: Littlefield Adams.

Politis, D. (2005). The process of entrepreneurial learning: a conceptual framework. *Entrepreneurship Theory and Practice, 29*(4), 399–424.

Rogers, C. & Freiberg, H. J. (1994). *Freedom to learn* (3rd ed.). New York: Macmillan.

Rossman, G.R. & Rallis, S.F. (1998). Learning in the field. London: Sage Publications.

Sarasvathy, S.D. (2008) Effectuation: elements of entrepreneurial expertise. Cheltenham: Edward Elgar Publishing.

Sarasvathy, S.D., Dew, N., Velamuri, S.R., & Venkataraman, S. (2005). Three views of entrepreneurial opportunity. *International Handbook Series on Entrepreneurship, 1*(Part 3), 141–160.

Schön, D. (1983). *Educating the reflective practitioner: how professionals think in action.* New York: Basic Books.

Scrivener, S. A. R. (2006). Visual art practice reconsidered: transformational practice and the academy. In M. Mäkelä & S. Routarinne (Eds.), *The Art of Research* (A 73). *Research*

Practices in Art and Design (pp. 157–179). Helsinki: Publication Series of the University of Art and Design.

Shane, S. (2000). Prior knowledge and the discovery of entrepreneurial opportunities. *Organization Science, 11*(4), 448–469.

Shaver, K. G., & Scott, L. R. (1991). Person, process, choice: the psychology of new venture creation. *Journal of Small Business & Enterprise Development, 16*(2), 23–42.

Sportlyzer (2010). *The Next Generation Private Trainer*. Retrieved March 25, 2011, from http://www.sportlyzer.com/.

Sportlyzer (2012) *About Us*, Retrieved July 21, 2012, from https://www.sportlyzer.com/.

Storkerson, P. (2009). Experiential knowledge, knowing and thinking. *EKSIG 2009: Experiential Knowledge, Method and Methodology* 19 June 2009. Retrieved July 21, 2012, from http://www.experientialknowledge.org.uk/proceedings_speakers_files/Storkerson.pdf.

Vygotskii, L. S. (1978). *Mind in society: the development of higher mental processes.* Cambridge: Harvard University Press.

Chapter 12
Wikipedia: Harnessing Collaborative Intelligence

Zann Gill

> *What use could the company make of an electric toy?*
> Western Union on rejecting rights to the telephone, 1878.

Introduction

Wikipedia, as an Internet-based innovation network that manifests distributed *collaborative intelligence*, illustrating principles for experimental venture laboratories and high return startup accelerators based less upon traditional directed innovation, more on intersecting networks and innovation clusters and the method being used in program development for a NASA initiated Planetary Sustainability Co•Laboratory.

Jimmy Wales, founder of *Wikipedia*, spoke at the Hult International School of Business in San Francisco about the experimental nature of venture creation, recounting how *Wikipedia* emerged from a series of failed business experiments, which included an Internet food ordering/delivery service, ahead of its time, and an encyclopedia (*Nupedia*) to provide free knowledge, funded by online advertising. These business failures formed a directed series of learning experiments, much as evolution in nature manifests direction toward increased functional effectiveness. *Wikipedia's* history encapsulates the experimental nature of successful new venture creation (Lih and Wales 2009).

Although on first glance the story of how *Nupedia* became *Wikipedia* seems like a series of accidents, *Wikipedia* arose from a logical sequence of experiments that

Acknowledging the innovative leadership of Sustainable Silicon Valley in building innovative links between new venture creation and smart systems for eco-cities to support a Planetary Sustainability Co•Laboratory (PS Co•Lab), engaging the collaborative intelligence of NASA, SSV, and other partners.

Z. Gill (✉)
NASA Ames Research Center & Sustainable Silicon Valley, DESYN Lab, 4001, Los Altos, CA 94024, USA
e-mail: zanngill@desyn.com

M. Curley and P. Formica (eds.), *The Experimental Nature of New Venture Creation*, 127
Innovation, Technology, and Knowledge Management, DOI: 10.1007/978-3-319-00179-1_12,
© Springer International Publishing Switzerland 2013

was far from accidental. Each failure informed the next experiment. Driven by a grand vision, a free encyclopedia that could bring knowledge to everyone, Jimmy Wales had a criterion, but no clear goal. From its beginning, *Nupedia* was a free content encyclopedia, aiming to generate revenue from online ads. Although the idea of delivering free knowledge to everyone was revolutionary, *Nupedia* followed the traditional model: To produce an encyclopedia, hire experts. After wasting $250,000 and producing only a few dozen articles, in January 2001 *Nupedia* started *Wikipedia*, initially as a side-project to generate more articles faster through collaboration, prior to peer review. Then came the breakthrough realization: distributed collaboration of many authors who did not know each other could itself constitute peer review, compressing the two stages of write/review into one. As *Wikipedia* grew exponentially, attracting more contributors, rather than remaining a low-level support system to generate articles faster, letting them rise to legitimacy through the slow *Nupedia* peer review cycle, instead *Wikipedia* grew exponentially, evolving independently of *Nupedia*. Not only had the two stages of article production and peer review been compressed into a single cycle, the entire process of vetting and posting had contracted to rapid, iterative A-PR (Autonomy | Pattern Recognition) cycles, the foundation for *collaborative intelligence* as described below.

Jimmy Wales ran short of cash in December 2001 and stopped funding *Nupedia*'s Editor-in-Chief Larry Sanger, who left soon after. From the ashes of the outworn encyclopedia model, the ancillary *Wikipedia* evolved into the core enterprise, exemplifying how new venture creation evolves through a continual process of experiment and revision (Wales and Weckerle 2008; 2009). Despite being a non-profit venture without online advertising, *Wikipedia* is highly successful at raising donor funding, and one of the most visited sites in the world. Its history embodies principles of new venture creation, applicable not only to effective nonprofits but also to for-profit start-ups and to change management in large organizations (Poe 2006; Wikipedia 2012).

Wikipedia itself emerged from a sequence of experiments and has procreated new experiments, such as *Wikia*. In February 2012, *Breaking News World* announced that *Wikipedia's* for-profit spin-off *Wikia* had close to 50 million unique monthly visitors, almost one-third of the traffic of *Wikipedia*. *Wikia* had proven the concept described in 2007 (McNichol 2007). From *Wikipedia* to mobile apps, from traditional service ventures to entrepreneurs commercializing the next hot gizmo, the experimental nature of venture creation is non-random. In both natural evolution and human innovation random variation plays a role. But the trajectory itself, the sequence and directedness of adaptation to feedback from experiments, is non-random. Each *Wikipedia* co-author is an experimenter, trying an article, gathering and responding to feedback from other editors about the last experiment. Each experiment builds on the previous, which elicits useful feedback. *Wikipedia's* history illustrates how experiments drive new venture creation. Six principles of *collaborative intelligence* underpin convergent experiments toward effective outcomes:

First, **collaborative autonomy** enables increasingly effective performance, whether in nature, innovation in new ventures, or world-class execution in large organizations.

Second, **performance criteria** take precedence over goals. Both new venture creation and change management entail managing high levels of uncertainty.

Third, **the critical path** of innovation is guided by the situation architecture of the context; pattern recognizers are local information processors, compiling data in context.

Fourth, **effective novelty** is the outcome of effective search, converging toward context-responsive solutions, both in natural evolution and in human ventures.

Fifth, **effective search** mirrors the capacity of evolutionary search to harness useful results through continual cycles of experiment, adjustment, and improvement, supported by next generation tools.

Sixth, **embedded Continual Assessment (ECA)** mirrors environmental selection as each experiment provides rapid feedback to guide the next (Gill 2012b).

Wikipedia demonstrates collaborative autonomy as each contributor brings unique motivation, skills, and knowledge to a shared framework. Performance criteria take precedence over goals as each article evolves, a work in progress, reassessed differently by each new editor. *Wikipedia* exemplifies how performance criteria take precedence over goals in new venture creation: Jimmy Wales had a clear criterion, delivery of free knowledge to everyone. But he could not specify his goal, the form that could successfully realize his criterion for success.

Distinguishing Collective from Collaborative Intelligence

When computer scientists adopted the term *collective intelligence,* giving that term a specific technical denotation, multiple connotations of *collective intelligence,* remained which led to confusion. A complementary term was needed to distinguish between anonymous homogeneity in collective prediction systems and non-anonymous heterogeneity in collaborative innovation networks (Gill 2011c).

Collaborative intelligence provides frameworks to harness our capacity for pattern recognition. Classic authors, such as Charles Mackay and Irving Janis, studied the negative impacts of crowd delusion, from market crashes to bad policy (MacKay 1852; Janis 1982). In Figure 1 the world symbolizes objectivity

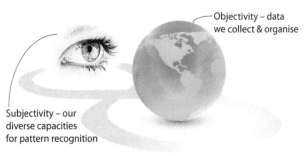

Fig. 1 Collaborative intelligence: data (the world) and pattern recognition (the eye)

Objectivity – data we collect & organise

Subjectivity – our diverse capacities for pattern recognition

Subjectivity – Objectivity Complementarity of *Collaborative Intelligence*

(the world of facts). But facts are not our only reality. The eye symbolizes subjectivity, our ability as pattern recognizers to interpret those facts. Many eyes on a problem world recognize different patterns and interpret those patterns differently. Facts integrated into effective knowledge networks build *collaborative intelligence*. A problem-solving ecosystem becomes an innovation network when it effectively taps each participant's unique perspective (eye on the world), skills, expertise, and problem-solving capacity to converge toward *collaborative intelligence*. Cross-disciplinary, distributed teams with critical time-related data contextualize information to be interpreted, enabling new venture experiments to be rapidly assessed.

Wikipedia authors have different perspectives, expertise, and capacity to write articles on different topics. An agent's utility function is an internal representation of potential fitness consequences of behavior. In this case, an agent is a *Wikipedia* author. Ecosystem utility for the whole system emerges as different agent utilities are reconciled, enabling *collaborative intelligence*. To distinguish between collective and collaborative intelligence requires distinguishing undifferentiated collectives from differentiated, distributed agents in computer–human networks. *Collective intelligence* aggregates input from large numbers of discrete, generally anonymous, responders to specific, generally quantitative, questions, using algorithms to process input from these responders to generate better-than-average predictions. In contrast, *collaborative intelligence* offers principles and frameworks to tap the diverse expertise of generally non-anonymous participants in a problem-solving process.

The A-PR Model Applied to New Venture Creation

Life's capacity to engage in A-PR (**A**utonomy | **P**attern **R**ecognition) bootstrapping cycles drives new venture creation, characterizing how variation can be harnessed in agile, next generation problem-solving networks where rapid feedback drives each next experiment.

Autonomy traditionally connoted self-control of behavior in living systems. As used here, autonomy is the capacity to act in response to signals, to alter one's behavior in response to information from the environment and feedback from past experiments.

Pattern Recognition, typically seen as a complex cognitive function, has mechanistic precursors, as when a key "recognizes" a lock that it fits through the morphology of "fitting." Nobel laureate Emil Fischer first used the key-lock metaphor to describe biochemical pattern recognition (Lichtenthaler 1995).

In A-PR (Autonomy | Pattern Recognition) iterative bootstrapping cycles, an autonomous agent (A) engages in pattern recognition (PR) in order to exercise autonomy and agency (A) to act (Gill 2011a). The process of new venture creation can be accelerated by harnessing A-PR cycles, crowdsourcing the collection and processing of data to support *collaborative intelligence*. First principle: Collaborative autonomy enables increasingly effective performance to emerge. Second principle: Performance criteria take precedence over goals. The unpredictability of specific attributes of the problem solution characterizes innovation. Through *collaborative intelligence* a goal state emerges that could not be defined *a priori*.

Fig. 2   The A-PR Cycle

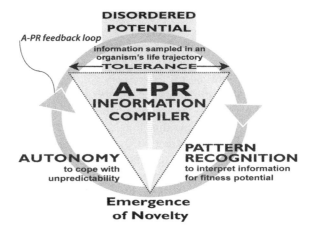

Figure 2 shows a single A-PR cycle in a self-improving system. Through iterative A-PR cycles, agents process diverse, jumbled signals and noise to filter, extract, and build coherent messages, coping with unpredictability and harnessing tolerance toward improved fitness and emergence of new capacities (Gill 2011b).

A-PR cycles are the bootstrapping engine through which individual utilities evolve toward Ecosystem Utility, starting from an agent's utility function as an internal representation of potential fitness consequences of behavior, which guides directed experiments. Animals, from bacteria to advanced mammals, process information, sorting signals to filter out noise, integrating data to converge toward useful messages. Living organisms continually compile multiple signals into messages to navigate their ecosystems (Ben-Jacob 2004, 2010; Gill 2012a).

Subjective perception rapidly translates into action in the world, becoming our next reality. Contrary to the traditional view that collaboration starts with consensus, *collaborative autonomy* allows contributors to retain ownership and responsibility, to keep their unique identities and diverse roles and priorities as they apply their particular skills as contributors in an innovation network. Contributors are not homogenized, as in consensus-driven processes, nor equalized through quantitative data processing, as in collective intelligence. *Collaborative autonomy* applies principles of evolutionary adaptation, overcoming the tendency of many processes to stall by requiring consensus (Gill 2013).

Lessons from Wikipedia

In 1995, Ward Cunningham introduced the concept of Wikis (Leuf and Cunningham 2001). From *Wikipedia's* launch in 2001, it grew exponentially, largely due to an exponential increase in the number of users contributing new articles. *Wikipedia's* open editorial policy made this exponential growth possible and was itself a surprising new venture experiment in scalability of a collaborative, networked enterprise. Understanding the behavior and motivation of *Wikipedia* "users as contributors" offers a window on *Wikipedia's* general evolution (Almeida et al. 2007). Despite general consensus that *Wikipedia*, one of the most trafficked Internet sites in the world, is a success, how to distill and translate the secrets of its effectiveness is exploratory.

Although *Wikipedia's* success is often attributed to the large numbers of contributors who improve the accuracy, completeness, and clarity of articles, while reducing bias, implicit coordination seems to play a key role in *Wikipedia* article development (Kittur and Kraut 2010). The importance of implicit coordination is a lesson from *Wikipedia* for experiments in new venture creation. New ways to map *Wikipedia*, using its socially annotated, hierarchical category structure (Kittur et al. 2009), suggest the importance of a structural framework to receive and organize unpredicted contributions. *Wikipedia* has evolved into a vehicle to facilitate collaboration (Miller et al. 2010), from which lessons about collaborative frameworks can be derived. Today there is less focus on how *Wikipedia* itself emerged, more on how *Wikipedia* can serve as a research tool to study the effectiveness of shared leadership in online communities (Zhu et al. 2012).

Wikipedia's success rests on distinguishing collective from *collaborative intelligence* as described above, enabling individual contributors to bring their unique, individual talents to collaborate with others whom they do not know, enabled by *Wikipedia's* collaborative framework. Translating lessons from *Wikipedia* to grow innovation networks can create new value, identifying synergies across products and services, and augmenting traditional incubators.

Entrepreneurs who participate in innovation networks have opportunities to test and showcase their products in integrated projects. System integration and total system performance monitoring can offer students real-world learning experience, producing resources and case studies for sustainability innovation curriculum. A global network of entrepreneurs can drive integrated applications, engaging universities, informal learning venues, and local citizen scientists to build global *collaborative intelligence*, powered by smart tools. Information sharing through a living lab "ecosystem" can be supported by an online showcase for outstanding product applications and model projects. By integrating innovation across exponential markets, such as Green-IT and Predictive Analytics, connecting entrepreneurs and products into testbeds for smart campuses, smart communities, and eco-cities, incubator networks can develop integrated technology solutions.

Crowdsourcing Innovation and New Venture Experiments

Venture capitalist Heidi Roizen predicts that the next wave of innovation may lie less in new technology, more in new business models and subtle shifts enabled by growing Internet reach and capacity (Roizen 2012). For example Method Products (non-toxic cleaning products) co-founder Adam Lowry is a Stanford-trained chemical engineer and climatologist who worked on the Kyoto Protocol. His $100+ Million company has changed the $5+ Billion cleaning products industry.

NASA Research Scientist in Artificial Intelligence Mark H. Shirley notes that to support continually more effective performance, a hybrid of social networks and crowd-sourcing platforms could become a fertile area of work: "Keeping track of the capabilities and experience of agents within a problem-solving network, and developing methods rapidly to assemble teams to solve particular problems, calls to mind the scene at the beginning of each episode of Mission Impossible where team-leader Phelps listens to his mission, then looks through dossiers of the available agents to select the best team for the task. How could a crowd-sourcing system most effectively perform this task? What skills would agents need to assemble into teams rapidly?" Shirley draws analogy to management consultancies: even those who do not use the term *collaborative intelligence* often apply its principles to improve their capacity to assemble effective problem-solving teams. Knowledge-sharing and knowledge networks examine problems associated with credit assignment and knowledge hording. Overcoming such problems to develop *collaborative intelligence* requires systems that support collaborative autonomy such that individual contributors are credited.

Three next generation tools categories can support *collaborative intelligence* in new ventures: next generation recommender systems, not only to recommend but also to solicit expertise (Li et al. 2011; Gill 2011c); next generation crowd-sourcing, not only to crowd-source basic microtasks but also to crowdsource pattern recognition (Ekstrand and Riedl 2011; Kim et al. 2011; Gill 2011c), by integrating from diverse responders to generate a complete message; and next generation social networks that go beyond profiling and sharing to support collaboration (Gill 2011a).

The term crowdsourcing was originally coined by Jeff Howe in an article in *Wired Magazine* to describe using the Internet to distribute microtasks (Howe 2006). Amazon's Mechanical Turk is an effective system to distribute microtasks to large numbers of autonomous, independent workers. Crowdsourcing precursors for *collaborative intelligence* tackle the integration challenges that arise from microtask distribution, such as collaborative search (Biewald, Microsoft *bing*), quality control (Biewald, Crowdflower), innovation (Spradlin and Bingham, co-founders of Innocentive; Kaufman, founder of Quirky), geographic data processing (Barrington and Lin, co-founders of TomNod), and community engagement in land use planning (Dinsmore, founder of Crowdbrite).

Lukas Biewald, while working on the Microsoft Search Engine *bing*, used Mechanical Turk to test how users evaluated responses to different search queries. This work made him aware of the need for a quality control layer to sit above the basic service of Mechanical Turk (Le et al. 2010). Biewald started the company *Crowdflower* to provide this service. He was also instrumental in starting the first conferences that encouraged researchers to work and publish in this field. From a handful of papers in 2008, there were close to 4000 papers in 2010, followed by exponential takeoff.

Founder Ben Kaufman launched his company *Quirky* with the vision to make it possible for anyone with a good product idea to get that idea developed and produced (Hart 2011). The online company *Innocentive* typically runs competitions where a contract is awarded to the best responder to a given task request. In some instances, it would be advantageous to identify a diverse set of superior submissions as partial solutions to a given problem, and to integrate what each Responder proposes to produce a complete solution. Collaborative intelligence entails capacity to aggregate and integrate results (Bingham and Spradlin 2011).

Luke Barrington and Albert Lin founded *Tomnod*, initiating a project to engage 6,000 *National Geographic* researchers to analyze satellite images, searching for hidden clues about the location of the hidden tomb of Genghis Khan. This analysis served as preparation for a *National Geographic* expedition to the wilds of Mongolia (Lin 2011). *Tomnod* has also used crowdsourcing to analyze earthquake damage, and for rapid response to address recovery needs (Barrington 2011).

Sheridan Tatsuno, founder of Silicon Valley Global Network, is a pioneer in understanding how collaborative intelligence can support smart, sustainable urban systems (Tatsuno 1986, 2012). Darin Dinsmore, a land use planner, saw inefficiencies in traditional planning methods and realized that a platform was needed for citizen participation in land use planning. His aim was to engage more effective community involvement in urban development by soliciting greater participation at reduced cost. He founded *Crowdbrite* (Dinsmore 2011). The City of Boston has pioneered experiments in urban monitoring that push crowdsourcing platforms toward data integration for *collaborative intelligence* (Reades et al. 2007). As applications scale up to engage large numbers of mobile device users, all monitoring their local areas, taking geo-tagged, time-stamped photos, a range of issues, from land use to safety to disaster response, can be addressed.

Embedded Continual Assessment

Methods are being developed to enable continual user assessment of the quality of *Wikipedia* articles (Dalip et al. 2011). Embedded Continual Assessment (ECA) in any new venture network should mirror evolutionary search, enabling rapid agile prototyping, with capacity for quick frequent interim feedback so that each experiment can guide the next. The paradox of prediction characterizes the uncertainty implicit in new venture creation (Gill 1986). The traditional view that we should first gather data, then analyze and predict market demand for each new venture, is supplanted by a model where quick experiments with embedded continual assessment provide rapid iterative feedback, so that each design drives the next experiment. The Internet is suited to such experiments; *Wikipedia* now provides more than a decade of proof that the system works.

To spin off new ventures, an innovation network must operate like a rapid responder system, with capacity to converge on, capture, and develop new venture opportunities. Rapid responder systems require simple heuristics for decision making, modeled on nature's methods for quick decision making (Gigerenzer 2010, 2011; Gill 2012a). To harness the *collaborative intelligence* of diverse participants requires better systems for semantic analysis, with capacity to cluster and link related concepts, visualize work in progress, tag user profiles, and credit individual contributions (Gill 2001). Because *collaborative intelligence* systems focus, not on predicting the future, but on pattern recognition in the present, they have a unique capacity to use *Wikipedia*-inspired online systems for new venture creation. Such systems typically require:

- **ontologies** for meta-tagging with a system to network and cluster meta-tags, not only to other like meta-tags, but also to similar, complementary meta-tags (a hard problem that requires human pattern recognition);
- **rating systems** for assessment, and filtering, so that more useful lessons learned rise to the top;
- **time-stamping**, so that expiry and critical path dates can be noted, and timeliness included in assessment;
- **authoring**, such that contributors are credited with a back-end system to track who contributed what;
- **search systems** that not only use key words but can also search parameter ranges, expertise and location of responders, date of incident and follow-up, clustering keywords and other search criteria to filter results, not only by topic but by estimated range of cost to implement, time to implement, team to implement, ROI etc.;
- **geo-tagging**, so that where incidents occurred, and which responder networks were activated, can be reviewed, and so that when new methods are pilot tested, results can easily be visualized;
- **incentives** to motivate responders to log incidents, meta-tag and rate results, both their own contributions and those of others, particularly those that most relate to their own;
- **rapid responder networks**, geo-temporal and based on bio-inspired design criteria to optimize speed of response, adaptability, and capacity for Embedded Continual Assessment (ECA) to trace and report on the status of emergency response in progress in order to optimize Responder Network performance, and
- **social problem-solving** capacity harnessing next generation networks, transformed into a problem-solving networks, with potential to scale and translate across varied requirements (Gill 2011c).

These performance capabilities are typically found in natural ecosystems. Irving Janis' pre-Internet research, from the 1960s to the 1980s, explored how committee-sized teams degenerate to foolish groupthink (Janis 1982). Although Janis' case studies were typically teams constrained to the number of individuals who could gather in a room to make decisions, his work merits review in light of current technology. Do his findings scale? Do they apply to large, distributed teams and to new venture creation via innovation networks? Wikipedia demonstrates that they do.

Conclusions

Wikipedia's development illustrates that the critical path of innovation must be vigilant, responding to the situation architecture of its context, tapping its users as information providers, and pattern recognizers to process information. Effective novelty, which for *Wikipedia* is defined as a good article, results from effective search, crowdsourcing to millions of potential producers of new content. Effective search attracts new authors to produce new articles as *Wikipedia* evolves, through ongoing experiments. Embedded continual assessment is implemented: content developers also serve as peer reviewers, editing content developed by others.

New venture creation, like rapid responder networks, must be agile, mirroring life's capacity as an information processor to perceive and respond to warning and opportunity signals. The method and tools of *collaborative intelligence* aim to systematize the means of "putting judgments together".

Dramatic technology failures reinforce the conclusions of Irving Janis' case studies, suggesting that effective support for *collaborative intelligence* in cross-disciplinary innovation networks could save billions of dollars and become a core venture start-up strategy.

References

Almeida, R. B., Mozafari, B., & Cho, J. (2007). *On the evolution of Wikipedia, ICWSM'2007 international Aaai conference on weblogs and social media.* Colorado: Boulder.

Barrington, L., Ghosh, S., Greene, M., Har-Noym, S., Berger, J., Gill, S., Yu-Min Lin, A., Huyck, C. (2011). Crowdsourcing earthquake damage assessment using remote sensing imagery. Citizen Empowered Seismology/Special Section In R. Bossu & P. S. Earle (Eds.), *Annals of Geophysics, 54*, 6. doi: 10.4401/Ag-5324.

Ben-Jacob, E., & Schultz, D. (2010). Bacteria determine fate by playing dice with controlled odds. *PNAS, 107*(30), 13197–13198.

Ben-Jacob, E., Becker, I., & Shapira, Y. (2004). Bacterial linguistic communication and social intelligence. *Trends in Microbiology, 12*(8), 366–372. 1 August.

Bingham, A., & Spradlin, D. (2011). *The Open Innovation Marketplace: Creating Value in the Challenge-Driven Enterprise.* Upper Saddle River: InnoCentive, Inc. FT Press.

Dalip, D. H., Santos R. L., Oliveira D. R. et al. (2011, June). GreenWiki—a tool to support users' assessment of the quality of Wikipedia articles categories and subject descriptors. In *Proceedings of the 11th Annual International ACM/IEEE Joint Conference on Digital Libraries* (JCDL '11), pp. 469–470, doi: 10.1145/1998076.1998190.

Dinsmore, D. (2011), Crowdbrite presentation. CrowdConf: November 1–2. San Francisco, CA; excerpt on Youtube: http://www.youtube.com/watch?v=JffxfrWUGeE.

Ekstrand, M. D., & Riedl, J. T. (2011). Collaborative filtering recommender systems. *Foundations and Trends in Human-Computer Interaction, 4*(2), 175–243.

Gigerenzer, G., Hertwig, R., et al. (2010). *Heuristics: The foundations of adaptive behavior.* New York: Oxford University Press.

Gigerenzer, G., et al. (2011). Heuristic decision-making. *The Annual Review of Psychology, 62*, 451–482.

Gill, Z. (1986). The paradox of prediction. *Journal of the American Academy of Arts and Science, 115*(3), 17–49.

Gill, Z. (2001). Webtanks: *Tools for Learning by Design*, SIGGRAPH 2001, Los Angeles, 292–296 (12–17 Aug).

Gill, Z. (2011a). Collaborative intelligence and effective complexity. In *Proceedings of the International Conference on Complex Systems*, ICCS 2011, Quincy, MA. http://necsi.edu/events/iccs2011/papers/317.pdf (26 June–1 July 2011).

Gill, Z. (2011b). The A-PR hypothesis: evolution at the threshold when non-life became alive. In *Origins 2011, Montpellier* (3–8 July).

Gill, Z. (2011c). Algorithmic implications of evo-devo debates. In *International Conference on Genetic and Evolutionary Computation*, GECCO 2011, Dublin. http://portal.acm.org/citation.cfm?id=2002097 (12–16 July).

Gill, Z. (2012a). A response to Darwin's dilemma: A-PR cycles and the origin of design in nature. In L. S. Swan, R. Gordon, & J. Seckbach (Eds.), *Origins of Design in Nature: A Fresh, Interdisciplinary Look at How Design Emerges in Complex Systems, Especially Life*, Dordrecht: Springer.

Gill, Z. (2012b). User-Driven Collaborative Intelligence—Social Networks as Crowdsourcing Ecosystems". In *CHI 2012 ACM SIGCHI Conference on Human Factors in Computing Systems*, San Antonio, Texas (May 5–10).

Gill, Z. (2013). The Other Edge of Ockham's Razor: The A-PR Hypothesis and the Origin of Mind. In: Biosemiotics. Special Issue "Origins of Mind" edited by Liz Stillwaggon Swan and Andrew M. Winters, Dordrecht, Springer. DOI: 10.1007/s12304-013-9176-6.

Hart, H. (2011). So you think you can design? *Quirky Tests Amateur Inventors*. http://www.wired.com/underwire/tag/ben-kaufman/. (Retrieved Feb 2012) (30 Aug).

Howe, J. (2006, June). The rise of crowdsourcing. *Wired*.

Janis, I. (1982). *Groupthink: Psychological studies of policy decisions & fiascos*. Boston: Houghton Mifflin.

Kim, S.-H., Li, S., Kwon, B.C., Yi, J.S. (2011). Investigating the efficacy of crowdsourcing on evaluating visual decision support system. In *Proceedings of the Human Factors and Ergonomics Society*, Annual Meeting September, *55*(1), 1090–1094.

Kittur, A., Kraut, R. E. (2010). Beyond Wikipedia: Conflict and coordination in online production groups. In CSCW 2010: *ACM Conference on Computer-Supported Cooperative Work*, New York: ACM Press.

Kittur, A., Suh, B., Chi, E. (2009). What's in Wikipedia? mapping topics and conflict using collaboratively annotated category links. In CHI 2009: *Proceedings ACM Conference on Human-factors in Computing Systems*, New York: ACM Press.

Le, J., Edmonds, A., Hester, V., Biewald, L. (2010). Ensuring quality in crowdsourced search relevance evaluation: The effects of training question distribution. In *SIGIR 2010 Workshop on Crowdsourcing for Search Evaluation* (CSE 2010) (23 July).

Leuf, B., Cunningham, W. (2001). *The Wiki Way: Quick Collaboration on the Web*, Boston: Addison-Wesley. ISBN 0-201-71499-X.

Li, W., Matejka, J., Grossman, T., Konstan, J., Fitzmaurice, G. (2011). Design and Evaluation of a Command Recommendation System for Software Applications. *ACM Transactions on Computer-Human Interaction, 18* Article 6 (July 2011), 35 pages. http://doi.acm.org/10.1145/1970378.1970380.

Lichtenthaler, F. W. (1995). 100 Years "Schlüssel-Schloss-Prinzip": What Made Emil Fischer Use this Analogy? *Angewandte Chemie International Edition in English*, *33*(23–24), 2364–2374.

Lih, A., Wales, J. (Eds.). (2009). *Wikipedia revolution: How a bunch of nobodies created the World's greatest encyclopedia*. New York: Hyperion. ISBN 1401303714, OCLC 232977686 (17 Mar).

Lin, A. (2011). National Geographic. http://www.nationalgeographic.com/explorers/projects/valley-khans-project/ (Retrieved Jan 2012).

MacKay, C. (1852). *Memoirs of Extraordinary Popular Delusions and the Madness of Crowds*. Bentley, London: New Harmony Books. 1980.

McNichol, T. (2007). Building a Wiki World. *CNN Money*. http://money.cnn.com/magazines/business2/business2_archive/2007/03/01/8401010/index.htm (3 Apr).

Miller, E., Seppa, C., Kittur, A., Sabb, F., Poldrack, R. A. (2010). The cognitive atlas: Employing interaction design processes to facilitate collaborative ontology creation. In *WWW 2010, Workshop on the Future of the Web for Collaborative Science*.

Poe, M. (2006). The Hive. *The Atlantic Monthly*, *298*(2), 86–94. http://www.theatlantic.com/magazine/archive/2006/09/the-hive/5118/2/ (Sept).

Reades, J., Calabrese, F., Sevtsuk, A., & Ratti, C. (2007). Cellular Census: Explorations in Urban Data Collection. *IEEE Pervasive Computing, 6*(3), 30–38.

Roizen, H. (2012). "A Running Start for Startups. Churchill Club", Microsoft Corp., (28 Mar 2012).

Tatsuno, S. (1986) The Techpolis Strategy: Japan High Technology and the control of the Twenty-First Century. NY: Brady/Prentice-Hall.

Tatsuno, S. (2012) In the Valley of Digital Dreams: From Farming to iPad in Silicon Valley. SF: CreateSpace.   http://www.barnesandnoble.com/w/in-the-valley-of-digital-dreams-sheriden-tatsuno/1111778075 ISBN 13:9781469969442.

Wales, J., Weckerle, A. (2008). Foreword. In M. Fraser & S. Dutta (Eds.), *Throwing Sheep in the Boardroom: How Online Social Networking Will Transform Your Life, Work and World* (1st ed.). West Sussex, England: John Wiley & Sons Ltd. Wiley, ISBN 978-0-470-74014-9.

Wales, J., Weckerle, A. (2009). Foreword. In L. Weber (Ed.), *Marketing to the Social Web:How Digital Customer Communities Build Your Business* (2nd ed.). Hoboken: Wiley, ISBN0470410973, OCLC 244060887 (3 Mar).

Wikipedia (2012). History http://en.wikipedia.org/wiki/History_of_Wikipedia.

Zhu, H., Kraut, R. E., Kittur, A. (2012). Effectiveness of shared leadership in online communities. In *CSCW 2012: Proceedings (in press)*.

Chapter 13
Business Model Experimentation: What is the Role of Design-Led Prototyping in Developing Novel Business Models?

Sabine Brunswicker, Cara Wrigley and Sam Bucolo

> *Today's business people don't need to understand designers
> better, they need to become designers.*
>
> Roger Martin, Rotman School of Management.

Introduction

Changes in today's global economic environment require firms to revisit traditional assumptions of the industrial era regarding how businesses create and capture value (Teece 2010). Thus, business models and business model innovation have been the foci of discussions in management practice and literature (Amit et al. 2010; Johnson et al. 2008). A technology is of little value if it is not commercialised via a differentiated business model. However, developing a novel business model to capture the value from technologies is not a trivial task, for start-ups or for established firms (Chesbrough 2010).

Existing practice-oriented case studies on business modelling highlight the central role of the 'value proposition' in order to link a technology to economic returns. In addition, the capability of business model experimentation is vital in order to identify radical new value propositions and business models, and to

S. Brunswicker (✉)
Fraunhofer Institute for Industrial Engineering, 70569 Stuttgart, Germany
e-mail: sabine.brunswicker@iao.fraunhofer.de

ESADE Business School, Barcelona, Spain

C. Wrigley
Queensland University of Technology, 2 George St,, Brisbane 4001, Australia
e-mail: Cara.wrigley@qut.edu.au

S. Bucolo
University of Technology, 730 Ultimo Rd, Sydney 2000, Australia
e-mail: Sam.bucolo@uts.edu.au

M. Curley and P. Formica (eds.), *The Experimental Nature of New Venture Creation*,
Innovation, Technology, and Knowledge Management, DOI: 10.1007/978-3-319-00179-1_13,
© Springer International Publishing Switzerland 2013

collect the data supporting it. The literature presents little understanding about how to facilitate business model experimentation (Chesbrough 2010). In design-led innovation, the iterative process of proposing 'radical new meanings', the act of creating visual representations, and prototyping are central. However, existing work on design and design-led innovation is not sufficiently linked to the concept of business model and business model experimentation (Verganti 2011). Therefore, there is a significant gap between both streams of literature and practice.

This conceptual chapter aims to bridge this gap in understanding by exploring how design-led innovation can facilitate the development of novel business models. To do this, the role of prototyping and artefacts in design-led business model innovation is detailed and explored.

In the following section, we review and critically discuss relevant literature pertaining to the concepts of business model innovation, experimentation, design and design-led innovation. From this, we discuss our research propositions and conclude the chapter with a hypothesised research agenda.

Business Model Innovation and Design Led-Innovation: Existing Literature and Conceptual Foundation

The term 'business model' is fairly ubiquitous and central to current management practice (Magretta 2002; Johnson et al. 2008). All businesses either explicitly, or, implicitly employ a particular business model that describes the value creation, delivery and capture of the mechanisms it employs (Teece 2010).

In existing literature, the concept of the 'business model' has been defined and referred to in various ways. These include; as a statement, a description, a representation, an architecture, a conceptual tool or model, a structural template, a method and so forth (Amit et al. 2010). While there is no single, consistent definition of what a business model is, there are key components. These components consist of; the notion of value (value stream, value proposition), monetary and financial aspects, aspects related to a firm's exchange relationships (e.g. delivery channels) and competencies and activities (Chesbrough 2006; Teece 2010; Magretta 2002; Zott and Amit 2010).

All in all, it is widely agreed that the notion of value is central to any business model (Teece 2010). A good business model needs to answer Peter Drucker's age old question: What does the customer value? (Magretta 2002). Innovation research shows, that answering this question is not a trivial task when developing a new business model. Further, scholars such as Zott and Amit (2010) emphasize that 'designing' business models is a crucial task for both entrepreneurs and managers. They discuss tools and methods such as an activity system framework to conceptualise a new business model.

From a technology and innovation perspective, the business model centres on creating and capturing value from investments in research and development (R&D); this is often neglected in reality (Chesbrough 2010). The economic return a business can expect from taking a new technology to the market is dependent on the business model. That is, the business model forms the heuristic logic that, in part, connects the technical potential with the realisation of economic return (Chesbrough 2006). To profit from innovation, firms not only need to excel in technology development and product innovation but also in business modelling and business model innovation (Teece 2010).

Chesbrough (2010) argues that a mediocre technology pursued with a great business model may be more valuable than a great technology exploited via a mediocre business model. Existing literature highlights that firms face significant barriers for business model innovation. This is due to a conflict between the established business model—within the firm or the industry—and the new one.

Prahalad and Bettis (1986) have highlighted the concept of the 'dominant logic', which relates to the main means a company endeavours to make profit and describes the cultural norms and beliefs that the company espouses. This logic represents a cognitive barrier for business model innovation. To succeed in business model innovation and to successfully link a new technology with economic success, management science literature emphasizes the importance of business model 'experimentation'. Chesbrough (2010) and Sosna et al. (2010) refer to case examples in various industries—ranging from music to pharmaceuticals. It is argued in business literature that 'experimentation' helps in conceiving a new business model and in generating the data needed to justify it. Furthermore, case studies highlight how business model innovation is not a matter of superior ex-ante foresight; rather, it requires significant trial and error, and quite a bit of ex-post adaptation (Chesbrough 2010).

Business Model Experimentation and Prototyping

'Experimentation' represents a scientific method that is widely used in empirical science. Experimentation is used to test existing theories or new hypotheses in order to support or disprove them. Scientific experiments require rigorous research planning and implementation in order to verify and validate a hypothesis based on empirical data and observations. In social science, in particular, experiments are regularly quite difficult to implement because important variables are difficult to control (de Vaus 2001).

The term 'experimentation' in the business model realm, has leant itself to the scientific notion of setting up experiments and controlling and manipulating certain variables of the business model. This process enables a hypothesised outcome to be tested through empirical observations of data (e.g. such as usage data, market share etc.). The term 'prototyping' is often used in business model innovation literature to emphasize the importance of the iterative learning and problem solving processes. This relates specifically to 'experimentation' when testing different solutions and adapting them based on the results of an experiment.

For example, Biddle (2012) poses the question; how do you prototype a business model? Based on this question, he provides a quantitative description of the various interrelationships of the business model elements—in essence, a financial model. The business model prototype serves a dual purpose. First, the prototype helps explore various scenarios and stress tests the viability (and profitability) of the venture. As importantly, it forces all potential assumptions to be stated.

Davenport (2009) states that too many business innovations are launched on a whim. She claims that this can be cured if companies provide investment in training, readily available software and the right encouragement. The organisation can then develop a "test and learn" capability. Companies that equip managers with the skills to perform small-scale yet rigorous experiments, not only save themselves from expensive mistakes—they also make it more likely that great ideas will see the light of day. The real payoff happens when the organisation as a whole shifts to a test-and-learn mindset (Davenport 2009).

Kijl and Boersma (2010) have developed a business model engineering tool that supports business model management as a continuous design, validation and implementation cycle. But by focusing on the design, implementation and evaluation of the business model the engineering tool treats business model experimentation in the pure sense of the definition of an "experiment". In controlling and manipulating certain variables to test a hypothesised outcome, the idea of 'experimentation' in a business model is reached.

The discussion on business model innovation indicates that the distinction between 'prototyping' and 'experimentation' of business models needs to be clear. We propose that the concept of 'prototyping' refers to the unlocking of a mind-set representing many future possibilities not just those you plan to implement. This allows for more than one concept to be held abstractly at once while bringing the concepts into the concrete as they are needed—becoming more of a learning and exploration process. When prototyping, the iterative learning and exploration of new business model options is the focus, as opposed to the testing of a predefined hypothesis. Existing literature provides insight into the importance of the trial-and-error process in the early stage of business model innovation. We argue that design and design-led innovation can significantly enhance a firm's capability to explore business opportunities and prototyping innovative business model options, without restricting the firm to a set of predefined alternative solutions.

Design and Prototyping

The benefits of early prototyping have been long recognised in the field of design. To provide a deeper understanding of the notion of prototyping in design, we first need to clarify what is meant by design.

The term 'design' is used by many disciplines to describe various activities. Over the years a plethora of studies (Yazdani 1999; Cross et al. 1996; Cross 2006) have described and defined the term in an attempt to further enhance and evolve the definition. Design can be used to describe a holistic and multidisciplinary problem-solving approach that takes user needs, desires and capabilities as its starting point and focus. However, design is not a linear process (Brown 2009). Design is categorised in the innovation field as the human-centred, prototype-driven approach, using designer's processes and frameworks to define and solve problems (Brown 2009).

The value of design is a different way of thinking, doing things and tackling problems from outside the box (Bucolo and Matthews 2011). Schön's (1983) reflection on action paradigm provides a particularly useful foundation to better understand the nature of design practice.

> *"A designer makes things. Sometimes he makes the final product; more often he makes a representation... He works in particular situations, uses particular materials and employs a distinctive medium and language.....There are more variables—kinds of possible moves, norms and interrelationships of these—that can be represented in a finite model. Because of this complexity, the designer's moves tend, happily or unhappily, to produce conse-quences other than those intended. When this happens the designer may take account of the unintended changes he has made in the situation by forming new appreciations and understandings and by making new moves. He shapes the situation, in accordance with his initial appreciation of it, the situation 'talks back' and he responds to the situation's reply. In a good process of design, this conversation with the situation is reflective. In answer to the situation's reply, the designer reflects in action on the construction of the problem, the strategies of the action or the model of the phenomena, which have been implicit in his moves"* (Schön 1983, p.78)".

It is the nature of the exploratory discovery, the production of unintended conse-quences and the reflection upon these consequences which point out the importance of prototyping rather than experimentation within the design process. The work of Polanyi (1998) and Ehn (1988) provide a further foundation to consider early stage or conceptual design activity, where discovery is intensified and can be observed. Both works (Ehn 1988; Polanyi 1998) refer to design as a process of making new discov-eries by constructing alternative futures. In all three approaches (Ehn 1988; Polanyi 1998; Schön, 1983) the interaction between the designer and their artefacts during this phase of design activity is seen as a contributor to discovery and new knowledge.

In Schön's (1983) initial description of the reflection on action paradigm he describes the sketch as talking back and revealing issues to the designer. Schön describes the evolving physical prototype as a more active and evocative par-ticipant than the sketch. This is because the prototype responds through physical behaviour, allowing the designer to obtain feedback through seeing, smelling and hearing. Stoll (1999) defines four types of physical models (artefacts):

- appearance models—communicating how the product might look;
- behavioural models—investigate how the design idea might be used or operated;
- functional models—how the concept may operate or perform its function; and
- design verification units—used to validate or confirm the final design.

Such artefacts are crucial in the design process and, thus, are highly important for 'prototyping' activities.

Erickson (1995) further defines categories of physical models. He argues that to be effective as a medium for interaction, prototypes should have two proper-ties—accessibility and the appropriate level of roughness. Any member of the team, regardless of location or skill level, should be able to modify the prototype. Roughness decreases the level of commitment to the design, therefore leaving the design team more open to considering change.

We propose that in business model prototyping, artefacts also play an important role and when prototyping business models, one may also categorise different prototypes. However, as opposed to products and services, there is a general lack of knowledge regarding the appropriate artefacts to prototype business models rather than tangible products.

The Strategic-Value of Design and Design-Led Innovation

Recent research indicates that companies who use design in their business, tend to perform better economically in the marketplace (Cox 2005; Borja de Mozota 2003; Dell'Era et al. 2010; Moultrie and Livesey 2009). Specifically, research by the UK Design Council, found that over a ten-year period of analysis the benefits of effective use of design include an improved share price performance and therefore greater shareholder returns (UK Design Council 2004). Furthermore, Cox (2005) identified that design enhances the outcomes of numerous innovation activities, bringing benefits such as increased quality of goods and services, improved production flexibility and reduced material costs. Design is increasingly being viewed as a vital and important strategic business resource (Dell'Era et al. 2010). Consequently, companies worldwide look to design to help them innovate, differentiate and compete in the global marketplace.

According to Verganti (2008) *'design driven innovation'* is a strategy that aims to radically change the emotional and symbolic characteristics of products and services through a deeper understanding of broader changes in society, culture and technology. Rather than being driven by user needs or technological developments, design-driven innovation is pushed by a firm's vision about possible new product meanings and languages that could diffuse in society (Verganti 2008).

Firms using design-driven innovation are competing through products and services that have a radical new meaning—those that convey a completely new reason for customers to buy them (Dell'Era et al. 2010). Dell'Era et al. (2010) identify design-driven innovation as innovation where the novelty of message and design language are significant and prevalent compared to the novelty of functionality and technology. This is based on the idea that each product holds a particular meaning to consumers and that the product styling is often used as a rhetoric tool to help communicate product value.

'Design-led innovation' describes a framework to culturally embed design within a business and to enable strategic and radical innovation. Design-led innovation therefore provides a unique opportunity for radical innovation in business value. This is because design-led innovation enables the generation of various propositions. This is achieved by using the designer's sensibility and methods to match people's needs with what is technologically feasible. From this the business can focus on a viable business strategy that can convert the proposition into customer value and market opportunity (Brown 2009).

In order to create and foster strategic innovation, designers continuously toggle back and forth between divergent and convergent thinking modes. They also operate both in the 'concrete' and 'abstract' world when prototyping (O'Mahony and Bechky 2008). Instead of directly moving from *'observations'* to *'solutions'*, designers make use of *'frameworks'* and *'imperatives'*. *'Observations'* are used to collect data about the real world. Further, design-led innovation relies on frameworks to *'reframe'* observations and develop a new problem statement. *'Imperatives'* translate the problem statement into a value proposition, but not the features or capabilities of the solution. These imperatives and ideas are then turned into *'solutions'* and *'artefacts'* (Beckman and Barry 2008).

The Design–Led Innovation Framework (Fig. 13.1) illustrates that within any business a continuum exists between operation and strategic activities and these activities have an internal and external focus. Different organisational groups and staff are tasked with these different activities and have specific key performance indicators (KPIs), dependant on their functional role within the organisation. Core to this framework is that to achieve strategic impact, any innovation can create change at all levels of the business. Therefore, a key objective of the model is to identify and design these changes at the time of conception rather than at launch. Within this design-led innovation framework the notion of the prototype takes on a new and extended meaning to what has been described by Stoll (1999) and Erickson (1995). The prototype in this instance is represented as the opportunity or proposition and becomes the bridge between the operational and strategic activities within the firm. This then links the internal and external stakeholders in the on-going development of the opportunity.

The business value proposition is central to the opportunity being considered. The prototyping that occurs, when following the framework, enables firms to challenge existing thinking. Design-led prototyping links the project as well as the

Fig. 13.1 The design–led innovation framework *Source* Bucolo and Matthews 2011

business perspective, thus, it enables firms to brake with the existing mental model and common beliefs about how firms create and capture value. In sum, the design-led innovation approach may provide the conceptual foundation for future investigations into the notion of business model prototyping.

Novel Business Models and Design-Led Business Model Innovation: A Proposition and Research Agenda

In order to create novel business models, prototyping is imperative. When prototyping the focus is on the iterative learning and exploration of new business model options rather than the testing of predefined set of hypotheses. Design and design-led innovation may significantly enhance a firm's capability to explore and prototype innovative business model options without restricting the firm to a set of pre-defined alternative solutions. Design enables business model innovation to make new discoveries by constructing alternative futures. Further, business prototypes and artefacts in different forms and levels of abstraction may enable business model 'designers' to toggle back and forth between the real and abstract world exploring radically new business model options.

To initiate a new research agenda, our five propositions are as follows:

(1) Design-led innovation facilitates business model innovation by conceiving novel business model 'propositions' that signify new 'meanings' for the customers.

From a 'technology' and 'functional' world view, problem solving moves from technological functions and solutions directly to observations (Thomke 2003). We propose that design-led innovation will help to reframe the problems and propose business model 'propositions' that 'mean' value for the customer. Design-led innovation may facilitate constant back and forth movement between the abstract and real world, across all dimensions of business models such as markets, pricing, delivery channels, resources, business relationships and so on.

Design-led innovation may begin with the comprehension of subtle (and unspoken) dynamics in sociocultural models, and also may result in proposing radically new meanings for how a firm creates and captures values (Verganti 2011). Further, it may help to challenge the existing and dominant business model in a firm's industry by linking new technologies to new 'meanings' with customers and partners. Thus, design-led innovation may enable new entrants in mature markets to 'disrupt' not just from a technology point of view but also from a business model standpoint.

Future research may address questions such as:

- What factors influence the conception of business model 'propositions' that 'mean' value for the customers and 'value' for the partners?
- How can we describe in more detail 'meaningful' business model propositions which link meaning, not just to a product or a service, but also to the business model (including a firm's value chain partners, pricing models etc.)?

(2) Design-led innovation facilitates business model innovation through the creation of new business prototypes. These exist in the real and the abstract world, and centre on using artefacts to make both the novel business model and the process of business modelling more tangible.

Thus, the conception and experimentation with novel business models is challenging. In business model literature, there are a variety of tools and frameworks used to describe and develop new business models (Zott and Amit 2010); some of them do so by creating visual representations (Chesbrough 2010; Osterwalder and Pigneur 2010).

Design-led innovation may significantly enhance existing tools used to create such representations of business models. As stated above, designers make use of various types of prototypes and artefacts in both the real and the abstract world. Design-led innovation makes use of tools to create representations of observations, ideas and solutions. Throughout the process of design various tools help to create 'tangible' representations of observations, frameworks, imperatives (or ideas) and the final solution. These tools are used to make the intangible tangible and help to move back and forth between the abstract and real world.

Future research may address such questions as:

- What are the categories of business prototypes and artefacts used for business model prototyping?
- What criteria can help to describe and classify the role of different prototypes used in creating visual representations of novel business model ideas?
- How might these criteria differ between prototypes in the abstract world and radical business model solutions in the real world?
- What tools are required to make the process of business prototyping more tangible?

(3) Design-led innovation facilitates and accelerates the process of prototyping and the exploration of 'disruptive' business models by engaging in 'deep' abstraction .

To explore 'novel' business models, firms need to challenge their existing beliefs about their business models; thus, prototyping is essential. As discussed above, design-led 'prototyping' refers to the unlocking of a mindset representing many future possibilities not just those a firm plans to implement. Design-led prototyping allows for more than one concept to be held abstractly at once while bringing the concepts into the concrete as they are needed. This then becomes more of a learning and exploration process. To explore the 'unknown', firms should not restrict themselves to a set of pre-defined alternative solutions.

Design-led innovation may facilitate the exploration of new business model options by moving further away from concrete and real world scenarios (Fig. 13.2) —allowing for the use of prototypes to test business model options in the abstract world. A 'deep dive' into the abstract world to explore unknown alternative solutions is essential in the early stages of the prototyping process. Design-led innovation may facilitate this process significantly.

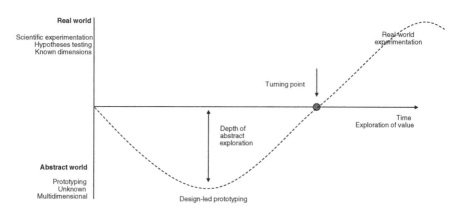

Fig. 13.2 Design-led prototyping in the abstract world and real-world experimentation

The design-led approach enables the consideration of the novelty and business opportunity as one, during the exploration phase. Whereas designers, traditionally, may only consider the idea in isolation, without framing it within an organisational and business context. In the design-led approach, designers move back into the real world and engage in what we call 'experimentation' and testing of predefined solutions.

Future research may address questions such as:

- What is the appropriate 'depth' of abstraction for business model prototyping to accelerate the process of prototyping without moving too far away from the 'real world'?
- How does this vary across different types of firms and industries? What is the right turning point (or multiple turning points for various aspects—see Fig. 13.2) when prototyping business model options?
- What is the relative role of artefacts for creating visual representations of radical business model ideas in the abstract world, throughout the process of conceiving and testing business model ideas?
- What is the role of prototypes in the "real world" respectively? How does the 'maturity' of the business model prototype (maturity as the level of details the prototype provides about the real business) influence the success of business model prototyping?

(4) Design-led innovation facilitates business model innovation with a new design capability and new functional role of designers.

Design and design-led innovation is about challenging existing beliefs, problems and solutions. Therefore, it is clear that design-led innovation may support the conception and testing of novel business models. This highlights the need for designers to function in parallel with corporate decision makers. This means the next generation of designers will need to be equipped with new capabilities and skills to enable them to engage with design-led business model innovation. These new designers will be familiar with models and concepts in strategy and business model innovation.

Further, design-led business model innovation may require new organisational capabilities and functions. For example, Norman (2010) proposes the idea of "transitional engineering"— a third discipline inserted in the middle of business and design—to translate between the abstractions and fuzziness of design through to the realities of business.

We propose that design-led business model innovation may also imply a set of new organisational capabilities to overcome the gap between the validity focus of business people and the creation of tension by designers. Traditionally business people are rewarded when budgets are met, hitting financial targets and proving in advance incentives will succeed. Using analytical tools such as linear regression to help them substantiate reliability on the basis of past results; if this has happened in the past, therefore it will happen again (for static and not dynamic environments). This contrasts with the notion of prototyping in the 'abstract world' and exploration of the unknown.

Future research may address questions such as:

- What organisational capabilities are required to engage in design-led business model innovation?
- What appropriate tools need to be used to close the gap between the traditional 'business world view' and the 'design world view'?
- What new skills do designers need to learn in order to engage in design-led business model innovation?
- What new functions and roles—such as transitional engineering—are required to enable design-led business model innovation?

(5) Design-led innovation facilitates business model innovation by engaging with customers and stakeholders and conceiving future value co-creation options.

Conceiving and designing novel business model value propositions requires firms to envisage future options of value creation and capture. However, in novel and meaningful business model innovations, value is not created by one single firm, it is created within the ecosystem of different stakeholders (Adner 2006).

Especially in services, value is co-created by a large number of stakeholders collaborating in a service system and contributing tangible and intangible assets and resources to the value creation process. Further, the 'meaning' of business models is not delivered but is also 'co-created'. Thus, designing novel business model propositions implies designing future 'co-creation' opportunities. Such opportunities may require the interaction and involvement with various stakeholders—including customers and complementary partners. Design-led innovation as a participatory and iterative process may facilitate this progression by proposing future value propositions to various stakeholders. This then helps in communicating value through the co-creation process and prototyping them in a collaborative manner (risk mitigation).

Future research in this area may centre on questions such as:

- What tools and frameworks are required to design future 'co-creation' processes?
- At what point in time should design-led innovation involve different stakeholder groups in business model innovation in order to propose new business value propositions?
- What are organisational contingencies for involving different stakeholders throughout the process of business model prototyping?

Conclusions

At this stage it is too early to draw any conclusions from the five propositions outlined in this chapter. Future research may build off the questions associated with the propositions detailed above. Exploratory qualitative and quantitative research methods may be used to garner a deeper understanding of how design-led innovation facilitates business model innovation and the value it generates.

This research will benefit scholars in areas of innovation and strategy, whether they come from design, management, technology or engineering. In the long run, conducting longitudinal analyses of business model innovation case studies may enhance the understanding of design-led business model innovation and its impact on the successful adoption and growth of new business models. This chapter provides a starting point, contributes to the discourse of design-led innovation and paves the way for this new stream of research.

References

Adner, R. (2006). Match you innovation strategy to your innovation ecosystem. Successful innovation requires tracking your partners and potential adopters as closely as you track your own development process. *Harvard Business Review, 84*(4), 98–107.

Amit, R., Zott, C., Massa, L. (2010). The business model: Theoretical roots, recent developments, and future research, Barcelona.

Beckman, S. & Barry, M. (2008). Developing Design Thinking Capabilities. *Academic Research Library, 24*(4), 24.

Biddle, B. (2012). Business Model Prototypes. from http://openopine.wordpress.com/2012/02/18/business-model-prototypes/.

Borja de Mozota, B. (2003). Design and competitive edge: A model for design management excellence. *European SMEs, Academic Review, 2*(1), 88–103.

Brown, T. (2009). *Change by design*. New York: HarperCollins.

Bucolo, S., & Matthews, J. (2011). *Design Led Innovation: exploring the synthesis of needs, technologies and business models, Proceedings of Participatory Interaction Conference 2011*. Denmark: Sønderborg.

Chesbrough, H. (2006). *Open business models*. How to thrive in the new innovation landscape: Harvard Business School Press, Harvard.

Chesbrough, H. (2010). Business model innovation: opportunities and barriers, *Business Models, Long Range Planning 43,*(2–3), 354–363.

Cox Review (2005). *The Cox review of Creativity in business: Building on the UK's Strategy*HM Treasury: London.

Cross, N. (2006). *Designerly ways of knowing*. Berlin: Springer Birkhäuser.

Cross, N., Christiaans, H., & Dorst, K. (1996). Analysing design activity. Chichester: Wiley.

Davenport, T. (2009). How to design smart business experiments. *Harvard Business Rreview, 87*(2), 68.

Dell'Era, C., Marchesi, A., & Verganti, R. (2010). *Mastering Technologies in Design-Driven Innovation*. March: Research Technology Management 53(2), 12–23.

Ehn, P. (1988). *Work - oriented design of computer artifacts*. Arbetslivscentrum: Stockholm.

Erickson, T. (1995). Notes on design practice: Stories and prototypes as catalysts for communication. In J. M. Carroll (Ed.), *Scenario-based design: Envisioning work and technology in system development, John Wiley & Sons* (pp. 37–58).

Kijl, B.,& D. Boersma (2010). Developing a business model engineering & experimentation tool—the quest for scalable ˍlollapalooza confluence patterns, AMCIS 2010 Proceedings.

Johnson, W., Christensen, M., and Kagermann, H. (2008). Reinventing your business model, *Harvard Business Review, 86*, 50–59.

Margretta, J. (2002). Why Business Models Matter. *Harvard Business Review.80*(5),86–93.

Moultrie, J.,& Livesey, F. (2009). *International Design Scoreboard: Initial indicators of international design capabilities*. Londan: University of Cambridge.

Norman, D. (2010). *The research-Practice Gap: The need for translational developers* (pp. 9–12). August: Interactions.

O'Mahony, S., & Bechky, A. (2008). Boundary Organizations: Enabling Collaboration among Unexpected Allies. *Administrative Science Quarterly, 53*(3), 422–459.

Osterwalder, A., & Pigneur, Y. (2010). *Business Model Generation — A Handbook for Visionaries, Game Changers and Challengers*. Hoboken, New Jersey: John Wiley and Sons, Inc.

Polanyi, M. (1998). *Personal Knowledge: Towards a Post-Critical Philosophy*. London: Routledge.

Prahalad, C., & Bettis, R., (1986). The dominant logic: A new linkage between diversity and performance. *Stratergic Management journal*, 7(6), 485–501.

Schon, D. (1983). *Educating the Reflective Practitioner: How professionals think in action*. New York: Basic Books.

Sosna, M., Trevinyo-Rodríguez, R., & Velamuri, S. (2010). Business Model Innovation through Trial-and-Error Learning The Naturhouse Case. *Long Range Planning, 43*(2–3), 383–407.

Stoll, H. (1999). *Product design methods and practices*. New York: Marcel Dekker.

Teece, D. (2010). Business models, business strategy and innovation. *Long Range Planning, 43*(2–3), 172–194.

Thomke, S. H. (2003). *Experimentation Matters: Unlocking the Potential of New Technologies for Innovation*. Boston: Harvard Business School Press.

UK Design Council. (2004). *The impact of Design on Business*. London: Design Council UK.

de Vaus, D. (2001). *Research Design in Social Research*. London: SAGE.

Verganti, R. (2011). Radical Design and Technology Epiphanies: A New Focus for Research on Design Management. *Journal of Product Innovation Management, 28*(3), 384–388.

Verganti, R. (2008). Design meanings and radical innovation: A meta model and a research agenda. *Journal of Innovation Management, 25*, 436–456.

Yazdani, B. (1999). Four models of design definition: Sequential, design centered, concurrent and dynamic. *Journal of Engineering Design* (0954–4828), *10*(1), 25.

Zott, C.,& Amit, R. (2010). Business model design: An activity system perspective. In: *Long Range Planning, 43,* (2-3)., 174–192.

Chapter 14
Taking Advantage of Experiments to Run Technology Companies: The Shimmer Research Case

Kieran Daly

> *His routine procedure seems to have been to start a novel with some structural plan which ordinarily soon proved defective, whereupon he would cast about for a new plot which would overcome the difficulty, rewrite what he had already written, and then push on until some new defect forced him to repeat the process once again.*
> Franklin R. Rogers 1966—Literary critic on Mark Twain.

Introduction

Shimmer Research is a technology company that designs and develops wearable wireless sensors, as well as developing algorithms to interpret the sensed world. By pairing the platforms and the algorithms together, we also provide a wide range of solutions that give real-time analysis and insight from 'data on the move'. Shimmer primarily operates in the health and sports areas and in this context kinematic and physiological data sources are the primary types of data analysed.

The original baseline platform technology was licensed from Intel in early 2008 to develop, market and sell the Shimmer platform globally. At that time, Shimmer was in use at Intel labs and a small number of external research groups associated with the Intel network. The technology was not commercially available and was instead loaned to partner institutes. We have worked to further the development of the platform technology and currently ship a version three revisions on from the original license.

K. Daly (✉)
The Realtime Building, Clonshaugh Business and Technology Park, Dublin 17, Ireland
e-mail: kdaly@shimmer-research.com; kieranfdaly@gmail.com

M. Curley and P. Formica (eds.), *The Experimental Nature of New Venture Creation*, 153
Innovation, Technology, and Knowledge Management, DOI: 10.1007/978-3-319-00179-1_14,
© Springer International Publishing Switzerland 2013

Shimmer Research is an autonomous division of Realtime Technologies and operates as a stand-alone business unit with our own team, bank, P&L, offices etc. Realtime is a privately held Irish multinational company in the contract electronic design and manufacturing business. It was established by Paddy White, who left Intel in 1996 to set up the company. Realtime is headquartered in Dublin with additional facilities in both the Czech Republic and Slovakia.

Shimmer Research is headed up by Kieran Daly and is headquartered in Dublin, Ireland with offices in Boston. Hardware development, software development and US marketing functions operate out of Boston. Sales, global marketing and application development are run from our Dublin offices.

From first customer ship in Q3 2008, we have established a user base in over 50 countries. With an annualised year on year growth rate of 70 % across the company's first 3 years of trading we hit our first breakeven month in Q2 2011. To date, we have shipped primarily into the academic and R&D sectors; however, we are now seeing growing traction from Original Equipment Manufacturers (OEMs).

As scale begins to gather pace, we are on target for over 300 % growth in the calendar year 2012.

The Vision of Shimmer Research is to be the global leader in the design and development of wearable wireless solutions and services.

How the System Works

Below is a graphical illustration of how the Shimmer platform works. Shimmer offers a range of sensing modules which can transmit or store the data for real time or offline analysis and interpretation.

Current Focus

The business has been bootstrapping thus far and what we understood to be our market in 2008 has altered significantly to where we operate today. This would not have happened by adherence to a 2008 business plan that projected the future in a dynamic market. Instead, through real-world experimentation, we have transformed into a much more robust, market ready entity that is positioned to scale.

Our current focus is on reinforcing our position as the market leader for wireless sensing platforms and solutions into academia and R&D whilst scaling and accelerating further business growth through sales of our solutions and sales to OEMs.

We are have evolved to target three priority markets:

- Research and Development, including Academic Institutes.
- The Solutions Market—Own brand Solutions.
- Original Equipment Manufacturers.

Summary Analysis for Each of These Markets

Research and Development

In the R&D market, the key driver of growth will be the educational market whereby the Shimmer platform is used as a teaching aid for labs in courses such as computer science, biomechanics and networking. The platform is in early stage use in two universities in Ireland for this purpose, and we are developing a shrink wrapped solution in this market for wider consumption. Added to this, we believe there is significant growth potential in the general R&D market that we are already serving.

Shimmer Research Solutions

The Shimmer Research Solutions business will be a key driver of expansion. Here we are working to release finished solutions to the market initially in the kinematics domain where we already have successes, particularly in elite sports monitoring and rehabilitation physiotherapy. This will transition the platform from its current profile as a general-purpose research tool to a fully fledged solutions-based suite of products with applications in both the sports and rehabilitation areas.

Original Equipment Manufacturers

The Shimmer OEM business is a volume-driven model where OEM's design in Shimmer as part of their own solution under their own brand. Margins are competitive in this model; however, this market is an important part of growing revenue and delivering scale that will help to drive down costs for the business as a whole.

Customers

Shimmers current user base extends to over 50 countries. Sales breakdown by geography:

- United States: 35 %
- Europe: 35 %
- Rest of World: 30 %

Currently, around 40 % of our customers are drawn from the research and academic areas. The balance is made up of industry and OEMs—including the R&D/product development teams within these companies.

Research and Development

The existing customer base includes many of the worlds Tier 1 R&D and Academic institutions as well as several notable OEMs. The research community is increasingly adopting the Shimmer platform and to date market growth is a blend of organic sales and sales driven from marketing leads. Shimmer Research has repeat orders from over 90 % of customers. Research clients include Harvard Medical School, Stanford, MIT, KTH (Sweden), TRIL (Ireland), Fraunhofer Institute (Germany), University of Wollongong (Australia) and JAIST (Japan), as well as corporate research labs at Samsung (South Korea), Nokia Labs (US) and Qualcomm (US).

This positions the platform for further growth in the well-defined and funded segment of healthcare research, and further validates our offering when engaging with potential industrial and OEM partners by referencing some of the high profile research and academic partners already in our client portfolio.

In the case of academic users, the average sales cycle is 10 weeks—down from 16 weeks originally, and we see continued improvement in sales cycle times through streamlined supporting documentation and more tailored product offerings. Typically, a research user would purchase an initial development kit, then, once evaluated, would purchase further sensors for in-house trials before scaling up to studies potentially involving 50–100 patients and/or end users.

Original Equipment Manufacturers

An increasing amount of OEMs are evaluating the platform. Currently, we have a number of integration projects underway. These will drive further scaling to the business. We have passed proof of concept stage with a number of the companies and are at various stages of putting commercial agreements in place. Examples of clients include Telefonica and Insight Diagnostics.

A notable OEM win is Telefonica, with whom we have developed a tele-rehabilitation solution called Rehabitic, aimed at patients who have had a total knee replacement and require extensive physiotherapy to recover. The solution allows their rehabilitation regime to be carried out in the comfort of their own home while maintaining the oversight of the clinicians who can monitor their session from the hospital. This launched in Q4 2011 in Spain, with a further launch across additional geographies in 2012.

Another OEM win is Emerge Diagnostics, an Oklahoma headquartered company headquartered company. In this case, we designed a wireless EMG system to replace their existing equipment. The Shimmer-based EMG is less than 1/4 of the weight of the original equipment and offers a more accurate EMG assessment due to its less restrictive nature. The Shimmer EMG has outperformed the legacy system and an FDA submission has been made with the Shimmer-based solution. We expect FDA approval for this solution in Spring 2013. This will further enhance the platforms appeal for other potential OEM customers and would assist in making the regulatory path more straightforward.

The sales cycle with OEMs is, on average, 12 months. The process takes broadly the same route as research customers:

- First Stage: Shimmer Development Kit Evaluation.
- Second Stage: Proof of Concept.
- Third Stage: Technical Roadmap development. Agreement on Commercial Terms.
- Fourth Stage: Tailored Shimmer Platform and/or Solution Development.
- Fifth Stage: Productisation and Commercialisation.

Marketing

In order to support our position and pricing, we are developing our marketing strategies from the following positions (Finkelstein et al. 2006):

Price	Features	Quality	Support	Access	Reputation
•Premium	•Original	•Excellent	•Comprehensive	•Restricted	•Prestigious
•Premium/ Competitive	•Original/ Customised	•Excellent / Average	•Comprehensive /Standard	•Restricted / Selective	•Prestigious/ Respected
•Competitive	•Customised	•Average	•Standard	•Selective	•Respected
•Competitive/ leader	•Customised / Basic	•Average / Acceptable	•Standard / Minimal	•Selective/ Universal	•Respected / Functional
•Leader	•Basic	•Acceptable	•Minimal	•Universal	•Functional

Currently, in terms of access, we are in the restricted/selective category—primarily as a consequence of our current customer base drawn from the R&D and academic community. We are moving towards the selective/universal area as we continue to enter into OEM agreements and develop our OEM customer base.

Of course, our reputation is enhanced by the halo effect from white papers and implicit endorsements by our customer base which includes leading universities, R&D Institutes and thinkers in the field of sensor technologies and biomedical research. These include universities such as Harvard and Carnegie Mellon University in the U.S., medical clinics such as Spaulding Rehab in Boston and St James' in Dublin and research centres such as TRIL in Ireland and KTH in Sweden.

We offer support that would be described as comprehensive/standard. In particular, at this early stage, we are keeping very close to our customers to get a better insight into their needs and concerns so as to inform the next generation of products and our technology roadmap.

The feedback from our client base is that the Quality and Reliability of the platform and service offering is excellent. These high expectations and requirements will continue—particularly in the context of our premium pricing model.

In terms of features, we offer both original and customised/bespoke solutions—R&D groups in particular require some original hardware depending on the application and it is important to support this need as it demonstrates the flexibility of the Shimmer platform.

Finally, on pricing the above attributes support a premium pricing strategy—this will tend towards the competitive section as we scale the volume side of the business in the OEMs market. However, it will remain premium in the lower volume, more specialised niche R&D and academic applications.

Thus, our target profile in the context of our OEM business development plan is:

Price	Features	Quality	Support	Access	Reputation
•Premium	•Original	•Excellent	•Comprehensive	•Restricted	•Prestigious
•Premium/ Competitive	•Original/ Customised	•Excellent/ Average	•Comprehensive/ Standard	•Restricted Selective	•Prestigious/ Respected
•Competitive	•Customised	•Average	•Standard	•Selective	•Respected
•Competitive/ leader	•Customised/ Basic	•Average/ Acceptable	•Standard/ Minimal	•Selective/ Universal	•Respected/ Functional
•Leader	•Basic	•Acceptable	•Minimal	•Universal	•Functional

2012 Onwards

Having refined our business strategy since startup—particularly over the last 12 months, and gained a deep understanding of the drivers and opportunities, Shimmer has decided on a simple yet highly effective approach to drive sustainable growth going forward.

What we provide is summarised into three offerings:

- Platforms.
- Services.
- Solutions.

Our target market segments (Fig. 1) are summarised as follows:

- Research and Development (R&D, and Academia)
- Shimmer Research Solutions aimed at appropriate niche markets.

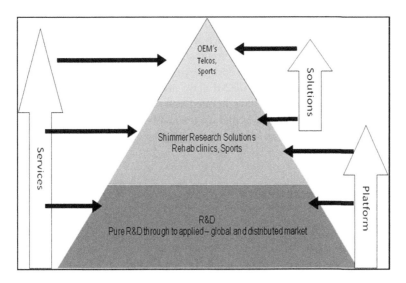

Fig. 1 Strategy pyramid: market segments and what we offer

- Original Equipment Manufacturers in the Healthcare, Sports and Convergence space.

  Market Segments
  We have segmented the market into 3 key areas, at a top level the segments are defined as follows:

- Research and Development—Researchers, Clinicians and Academics, who use Shimmer to further their clinical understanding and research goals. We aim to continue to build on the success to date in this segment. We offer Shimmer Platform and Services.
- Shimmer Research Solutions—Develop shrink wrapped, Shimmer branded solutions based initially on Kinematic applications. We offer Shimmer Platform, Services and Solutions.
- Original Equipment Manufacturers—Design in Shimmer to OEM solutions. Shimmer is the technology driver under the hood of the end customer's offering. This is a volume-driven business with more competitive margins. We offer Shimmer Platform, Services and Solutions.

Experimental Approach

A key element of Shimmers' success to date has been the experimental nature of our product offering, pricing and market selection strategy.

Many startups describe their small size as a benefit when entering new markets as it allows them to remain nimble; however, this agility is not always used to advantage. Shimmer was determined from the outset that this attribute would not be just a potential benefit and instead from our first product shipment we would strive to move fast and turn faster if circumstances changed.

The strategy pyramid was derived following three years of trading—not as an initial goal to work towards. As of 2012, we are in a very different business than we had initially projected. We have iterated several business plans and rather than sticking rigorously to these blueprints we instead began to rewrite the plans based on what we had evidence was being or becoming successful.

The Enclosure Example

From the time of signing the licensing deal with Intel to our first product shipment 5 months later we had to build our proposition, establish a channel to market and also carry out "bullet proofing" of the technology to make it market ready. Up to this point, the technology had not been commercially released. Once we began to charge paying customers for it, we understood that an improvement in the integrity and consistency of the hardware was required.

There were several trade off decisions to be made as our aim was to have the product released by the time the academic year began around September. This meant we had to develop a sales pipeline immediately after the Intel agreement even though we did not have product to sell at that point.

A tangible example of our experimentation approach can be evidenced in the in the evolution of our product enclosure.

From visiting some of the existing non-commercial users, we built up a profile of our target market and began to map out their needs. It became clear that aesthetics were not central to their purchasing decisions and accordingly we focussed on the technology element of our offering. This meant we reduced effort around the product packaging and enclosures. Our first products shipped in a modified off-the-shelf electrical enclosure box which was fixed in a single corner by a metal screw. Far from a slick looking device, the sensors had a distinct "maker" feel to them albeit that in terms of actual electronics it was a very sophisticated piece of technology.

By taking such decisions, we did succeed in getting product released and sold in line with the start of the academic year. As we looked toward improving the overall customer experience, we then gathered up all of the feedback from users regarding the enclosure which fed directly into our design roadmap for the next revision which we launched in mid-2009.

The 2009 revision included minor hardware improvements but significant changes in terms of enclosure and supporting documentation. We knew that our market was growing and also the type of customer we served was evolving from computer science-oriented research towards more patient-centric healthcare and sports research. At this progressed aesthetics became more important. We still felt that one more iteration was needed before moving to more formal industrial design and associated tooling costs of producing bespoke enclosures.

The 2009 revision was manufactured via a CNC process in see through plastic. A slightly curved edge was our only nod to aesthetics although we did reduce the overall form factor by eliminating the unused space associated with the electrical box enclosure. This time we included two screws diagonally opposing, to give a more robust feel to the sensors.

By 2010, Shimmer's client base was expanding and we were very conscious that some of our competitors who were less technologically capable were beginning to gain traction through their superior industrial design.

We knew the product offering did not match our ambition in terms of overall user experience and armed with two years of user feedback made the decision to engage formal industrial design expertise and associated capital spending on tooling/moulds.

As of 2012, we are preparing for the next generation of enclosures to match new and additional hardware releases. These will continue the aesthetic theme of the current design but also include functional elements that can be used as differentiators in a dynamic market.

In a less experimental model, there would be a temptation to have all of the enclosure considerations addressed before shipping any product. In our view, the most important goal was to win customers even if this was a small amount to begin with, then learn from them and inform technology, product and overall company strategy.

Reference

Finkelstein, S. Harvey, C., & Lawton, T. (2006). *Breakout strategy: Meeting the challenge of double-digit growth*. London: McGraw-Hill Professional.

Index

M. Curley and P. Formica (eds.), *The Experimental Nature of New Venture Creation*,
Innovation, Technology, and Knowledge Management, DOI: 10.1007/978-3-319-00179-1,
© Springer International Publishing Switzerland 2013

Lightning Source UK Ltd.
Milton Keynes UK
UKOW07n0942301014

240767UK00001BA/19/P